How To Ask God

for What He Wants to Give You

Bill Simpson

ISBN-13: 978-0-692-80841-2

Additional Small Group resources can be found at:
www.HowtoAskGod.com

Cover Design: Todd Phelps

DEDICATION

There is no one who has been more important to me than my dear wife and best friend, Tammy. This book is dedicated to her, for her unwavering and wholehearted commitment to our Lord, to our family, and to me throughout our incredibly adventurous life. Many others have taught me rich truths about following Jesus, but no one has shown me what devotion to God looks like the way she has. I also dedicate this book to our incredible children, Josh and Hannah, who are fervently committed and a joy to be with, and to their wonderfully faithful spouses, Mandy and Theo.

ACKNOWLEDGMENTS

Becoming a follower of Jesus happened by God's grace through the ministry of Dr. David Chadwick and the family of Forest Hill Church in Charlotte, NC, after listening to countless seed-sowing sermons from my father-in-law, Rev. C. Paul Jones (while dating his daughter). Dr. Dennis Gill of Community Bible Church was instrumental in guiding us to attend Columbia International University for theological training. My faithful professors at CIU and Reformed Theological Seminary, and our fellow servants at SIM International have all been strategic in shaping my understanding of God and how to have a vibrant and authentic relationship with him. I also want to acknowledge the enormous clarity I gained from Dallas Willard's books, especially *The Divine Conspiracy* and *Living in Christ's Presence.*

After returning from our ministry in Senegal, West Africa, I was honored and privileged to pastor two wonderful church families: Community Bible Church in High Point, NC and Manchester Creek Community Church in Rock Hill, SC. I am deeply grateful to both of these church families for the agape love Tammy and I received from them as their Senior Pastor.

I am greatly indebted to four gracious people who proofed and edited this manuscript: My dear wife, Tammy, our precious friends, Ruth Harris and Cindy Genung, and a brand new friend, Susan Yablonski. I thank each one of you for your diligent work and for your commitment to excellence. Ruth, you are the queen of formatting!

Todd Phelps leveraged his tremendous talent and worked so selflessly in designing the book's cover and in shooting and editing the promotional video. Thank you for your agape love my friend.

CONTENTS

Chapter 1 - Our Guide to Asking God

Let's change how you pray.

In order to improve our tomorrows, we have to make an accurate assessment of today. Answer these next three questions very honestly. Do you pray enough? Do you ask God for the right things? Do you pray in confidence, believing he will answer what you ask? Very few followers of Jesus think that they pray enough. Many also wonder if they're asking for the right things, which means they don't have a lot of faith that God will hear and grant their requests. Why is that? Why is praying to our Father in the heavens, who loves us more than we can possibly fathom, so challenging? And why are many of us undisciplined with our praying?

Praying is simply talking with our Father who longs to hear from us. But most of us lack the confidence that we know *how* to talk with him. We often feel like our requests are not worth God's time. We also get confused on what we should and shouldn't ask him. We believe he answers prayers, but we struggle believing that he will answer our specific prayers. If you had more confidence that your requests were important to God, how might that change how often you pray to him? If you knew without a doubt that he always listens to your every request, how might that change the way you pray to him? Let's face it, we could all use more confidence in knowing what God wants us to ask of him.

Children often pray with confident honesty: "Do animals use you too or is there someone else for them?" "Is Pastor Johnson a friend of yours or do you just know him through business?" Thank you for my baby sister, but I asked for a puppy!" "It made my dad really mad when it rained our whole vacation. He said things about you that people shouldn't say, please don't hurt him anyway, signed, your friend, but I'm not gonna tell you who I am."

Jesus came to show us who his Father really is, what he is like and how to have a meaningful and personal relationship with him. Relationships are always dependent on conversations. That's why Jesus prayed to his Father all the time. If *he* continually talked with his Father about all of his life's challenges, then *we* certainly need to do the same. And Jesus knows it's not easy for us. After all, he knows us better than we know ourselves. He knows that we lack assurance in praying. He knows you fall asleep sometimes when you pray. He loves you even when, after praying for two minutes, your mind is fixated on if it's time to change the oil in your car or if you paid your cell phone bill. It happens, right?

Who is one of your closest friends? How often do you talk, text or email them? What makes your friendship work? Isn't it honest and open communication? Don't you enjoy sharing your life, both the good and the bad, with your friend? What if you began to have a similar kind of relationship with your heavenly Father?

Relationships take effort. You can't have a solid relationship with God and not pray. It's just not possible. It is your responsibility, as a follower of Jesus Christ, to learn how to communicate in confidence with your heavenly Father. This is a learned behavior, which is why we readily join in with the disciple's request in Luke 11:2, "*Teach us to pray...*" This book is about building the kind of confidence that will launch you into regular and vibrant conversations with God. We will explore how Jesus taught his followers to pray so that we can grow in our confidence to develop an authentic habit of conversing with our Father in the heavens about what matters to us and to him. You are about to learn, directly from the Bible, how God wants you to pray and what he wants you to ask him to do.

How important is bread?

In Luke 11, Jesus taught his disciples an outline for praying. We typically call it "The Lord's Prayer". It is also found in Matthew 6:9-13. Maybe you memorized it and have been reciting it verbatim. Before we examine what Jesus taught us from that prayer, let's think about the story and the analogy he told immediately following that teaching. Both hold important keys for us to understand critical aspects about talking with our heavenly Father.

In the story, a visitor comes late at night and the man has no food for him. So he wakes his neighbor to borrow some bread for his guest but the neighbor isn't very happy with the request. He would wake his whole family if he got up to get his "friend" some bread and apparently their friendship wasn't real tight! Jesus' story reveals that the only reason the bread was given was because the man was so annoyingly persistent. He hounded his neighbor to the point where the guy was ready to *give him whatever he needs.* (Luke 11:5-8) Great friend, huh?

Jesus' point is that persistence is really important when praying to God. Jesus told another story to emphasize how much his Father values diligent determination. In Luke 18:1-8, a widow is bugging a judge to death about giving her justice against an adversary. She finally wears him down so that he gives her what she wants.

Jesus' point in both of these stories is definitely *not* that we have to find a way to wear down the Father. He is helping us to see, that if it is really important to us, we need to talk to God about it. We need to continue to ask him for his help. Jesus is also building our confidence in our asking because the reluctant friend and the unjust judge are completely opposite to God's character. How much more does God want to help us out in our time of need?

How important was the bread to the man who had a midnight caller? It wasn't a life and death matter. They both could have waited until the markets opened in the morning. Because of their friendship, it was important that this man give his worn out and hungry fraternity brother something to eat, right then. Friends don't let friends go to bed hungry! So he risked his other friendship, with his next-door neighbor, to wake him up.

In the grand scheme of things, it seems odd that Jesus chose a story about a non-life threatening need. It's not like he was demon possessed or lying by the roadside, robbed and beaten (Luke 10:29-37). The guy was hungry! He wanted something to eat.

Jesus followed the story with a startling teaching that his disciples had already heard: *"And I tell you, ask and it will be given to you; seek, and you will find; knock, and it will be opened to you. For everyone who asks receives, and the one who seeks finds, and to the one who knocks it will be opened.* (Luke 11:9-10)

Jesus doesn't mean that we're to ask and seek and knock one time. The entire context of his teaching is focused on our persistence. So the question for us, regarding our part in praying to our Father in the heavens, is this: Do we really want it? Is it so important to us that we will continue to bring it up in our regular conversations with our Father?

God loves to give us what's good

Next, Jesus emphasized his Father's part in prayer. And this is by far the best part of the passage. It also shows us that Jesus had a great sense of humor. He enjoyed making his disciples laugh!

"What father among you, if his son asks for a fish, will instead of a fish give him a serpent; or if he asks for an egg, will give him a scorpion? (vs11-12) Can't you picture Jesus cracking a big God-shaped smile while giving this super-exaggerated illustration.

When my son used to ask me for a Happy Meal, and that was daily, I never gave him d-Con pellets to munch on. When he asked for a Wendy's frosty, I didn't give him some ice-cold Round-Up! I met his need (although the Happy Meals were purchased with much less frequency than requested.) As parents, we love to give our kids what they need and want, at least most of the time.

How much more does our Father in the heavens want to meet our needs? Since he knows what we truly need, in every situation, he is the perfect one for us to ask to meet those pressing needs. Because we don't often know what's truly best for us or for others, it's very important that we keep on asking and keep seeking and keep knocking so that during this process, we can learn from God what actually is best. We may have the request just right. What you are asking for may be exactly what God wants to give you, but the timing isn't quite right. That's why persistence is required. You have to learn how to trust your Father's timing as well as his decisions about what is best and if your request is good for everyone involved.

Jesus admits that all of us fathers are lacking in goodness. He even calls us *evil*. He deliberately chooses these words because he is using the power of contrast once again. We earthly fathers know how to give good things to our kids, and we usually work hard to give them the best. I loved giving my kids what they wanted, as long as I believed it was good for them. In parenting, sometimes much wisdom is needed to know if our child's request is truly good for them or not. How much more does our Father, who is perfect love, want to give us what we truly need, his absolute best?

Jesus' crescendo to his teaching in this passage comes at the end of v13 when he concludes; "*how much more will the heavenly Father give the Holy Spirit to those who ask him*!" The very best thing that God could ever give to you is his Spirit. And he freely gives his Spirit *to those who ask him*!

How does the Spirit meet your needs?

"Now hold on Jesus. You gave an outline about praying and immediately told a story of a man who's need for food was met by his persistence. What does all that have to do with the Holy Spirit?"

I'm so glad you asked! Jesus' analogy is powerful, even

if it is a little fuzzy at first. Just as the man's midnight guest needed food, you and I need the Spirit to meet all of our needs. The Spirit of God has everything you will ever need for the rest of your life! That's right. He has all the answers to all of life's questions including each one of your specific questions about the details of your life and relationships. He knows everything about everything including everything about your past, present and future. There isn't anything that the Spirit of Jesus doesn't know about you and your life, your work, your family, your health, everything. He knows quantum physics, automobile repair and the intricacies of every Microsoft Office product. He knows how your cell phone works and where you put your glasses. He knows all the details of each one of your relationships and what every person is thinking and planning. The Spirit, like the Father and the Son, is all-knowing.

The Spirit knows all about your relationships. He knows what is needed in your marriage to make it all you both dreamed it would be. Jesus' Spirit knows who you should date and who you shouldn't. He knows how your co-worker will react to the email you need to send them about the problem in the office. The Spirit of God knows the results of the scan before your doctor even orders it. The Holy Spirit knows the beginning from the end and everything in between. He is our resource for all of God's strength to flow into our hearts and minds.

This is true for all who have been rescued by God and drawn to faith in Christ through the power of the Spirit. You are saved. Once you have been forgiven of all your rebellion against God, past, present and future, you belong to him. Jesus put it this way; "*All that the Father gives me will come to me, and whoever comes to me I will never cast out.*" (John 6:37) I highly recommend you study this

: 6th chapter of John on a regular basis.

nce we are made his by his goodness and grace, life is all about being transformed into people who think and act like the Lord Jesus. The technical word for this is sanctification. Therefore, once you come to believe in Jesus as God's Son and your Lord, all you need is more and more of the Spirit's power and influence in your life. It's not that we need more of the Spirit, like we begin with 25% and hopefully increase from there. It's that the Spirit needs more of us. When Jesus said that the Father longs to give us the Spirit, he meant that the Spirit will be a greater and greater force in our lives.

When Jesus first taught the model for prayer, what we call "The Lord's Prayer", in Matthew 6, it was very early in his public ministry. The scene in Luke 11 is likely about two years later. Jesus is with his disciples, not the crowds, and they understand him much better. Jesus reveals more to them now than he did before because they were not yet ready for it. They are still foggy about many things, but Jesus knows it is time to help them, and us, see that our true need is to align our lives more and more with his Spirit.

He is your helper

Jesus' Spirit is also our *Helper* (John 16:7-15), which literally means that he is the one who comes alongside us. As he comes along beside us he empowers us to love those who are difficult to even like, to overcome all kinds of temptations, to stand strong in our beliefs and convictions, and to know how to patiently tolerate annoying personality types. The Spirit is the one who can embolden you to tell others about the hope you have in Christ, to answer his leading to do certain things, to remember God's words and how to apply them to specific situations and to obey all that Jesus taught. It was the Spirit who drew you to believe in Jesus, to understand your sinfulness and his sacrifice, and it is the Spirit who guides your every move in life. If there's one thing in your life that you need above all else, it is the Spirit of Jesus guiding and leading and strengthening you.

As the apostle John neared the end of his extraordinary long life, he wrote; *By this we know that we abide in him and he in us, because he has given us of his Spirit.* (1 John 4:13) We remain as followers of Jesus because of the Spirit's help and presence within us. *You know him for he dwells with you and will be in you.* (John 14:17b) When Jesus promised that he would never leave us or abandon us, he wasn't referring to himself literally, but to his very Spirit. That's also why Jesus said that it was even better for his disciples that he return to the Father so that the Spirit could then come to be in them. Having the Spirit in us is better than hanging out with Jesus!

This is why Jesus concluded this profound teaching on prayer with the promise that his Father will *give the Holy Spirit to those who ask him.* How often do you ask the Father to give you his Spirit? How much are you depending on the Spirit's help for your life's challenges? The secret to fully enjoying the abundant life that Jesus came to give you is found in your daily dependence on the Spirit of God to strengthen you in the core of your being.

How many times is enough?

Jesus gave us an amazing promise. If we will ask the Father, and keep on asking, he will give us all we need. When we seek him and keep seeking him for his help, he will lead us to his answers for our circumstances and situations. When we knock and keep on knocking, he will open the doors that he wants us to enter, and he will close the doors that are not right for us. So when is enough, enough?

Persistence is part of learning how to be a follower of Jesus. The man in Jesus' story didn't stop knocking on his neighbor's door until he had what he wanted. The old widow didn't stop pestering the judge until she had what she wanted. Isn't Jesus implying that we are to keep asking and seeking and knocking until we get what we need? And the contrast is critical between the sleepy neighbor, the ornery old judge and our Father in the heavens. If the neighbor and the judge finally caved in, how much more will our loving Father give us what he knows is the absolute best for us? Don't stop asking him!

Do you remember when you were a kid and all you could think about was that gift you wanted for your birthday or Christmas? Maybe it was a bike or a doll. For me, it was a drum set from Sears that included a Ringo Star wig! Yes, I became a Beatle! What did you do to ensure you'd get it? You pestered your parents to death. I bugged my poor mom every day about my Christmas dream, that drum set, beginning in early October. I was sure that I knew what was best for me. Funny how I never considered how me banging on a drum set in our home might not be the best thing for the other five residents. Didn't you ask and keep on asking, hoping your persistence would convince your parents that they really needed to buy you that gift?

Jesus is making a bold contrast between the reluctant friend and his heavenly Father who loves us enough to sacrifice his Son. How much more does our Father want to use his unlimited resources to give us his best? The friend was very reluctant to get up but our Father is more than willing. The judge only helped the widow because she wore him out, not because he was just. Our Father never sleeps or grows weary and he is only just and faithful.

Jesus' prayer outline brings us into understanding of what we truly need. On so many occasions, I have asked the Father to do certain things for me or others, only to find that as time passed and I continued to ask, my request changed. The more I prayed the more clarity he brought to my mind and the more I understood what was truly needed. The more we grow in dependence on the Lord, the easier it becomes to discern how the Spirit is leading and what we should be requesting from the Father. As you continue being honest with God, you will realize how he is shaping your heart to know how to want the things that he longs to give you, that which is his best and highest for you.

Continuing to ask him is a tangible expression of how much you need God. I continued to ask my parents for the drum set because they were the only ones who could buy it for me. I had very little income at 8 yrs. old. I needed them to answer my request. They were my only hope. That's how persistence works with God.

If you are fine on your own, let's say with a problem at work, you'll simply land on the solution that works for you and go for it. But if you are living in dependence on the One who knows all things, you will incorporate him more and more into your plans and problems to seek his answers and to have him open the right doors. Aren't you tired of kicking in doors for yourself? Wouldn't you rather learn to wait for the Father to open them for you, when the time is just right?

In expressing our absolute need for God to help us, Peter encouraged all followers to stop acting independently and instead to cast all their anxieties and concerns on God. The word for "cast" is very literal. It's what you do when you throw your clothes on the bed. Why are we instructed to throw our burdens on his shoulders? Because he cares deeply about the things that weigh his people down. (1 Peter 5:6-7) God is the only one qualified to relieve your burdens, so he instructs you to throw them on him as you are praying.

In a similar passage, the apostle Paul wrote to the believers of the church in Philippi to face all anxieties and worries through prayer. As you persistently pray about the things that trouble you, because you are relying on your loving Father, his peace will guard your emotions and guide your reasoning: *The Lord is at hand; do not be anxious about anything, but in everything by prayer and supplication with thanksgiving let your requests be made known to God. And the peace of God, which surpasses all understanding, will guard your hearts and your minds in Christ Jesus.* (Philippians 4:5b-7) Notice how prayer is set in the context of an intimate relationship with God the Almighty; *The Lord is at hand.* He is here. Because he is present in your hardship, you don't have to be anxious or worried because you can unload on the Almighty. His peace will guard your emotions and your thinking as you learn to rely on him through your praying about the situation. Worry will likely return and when it does, pray some more, until the Lord's peace returns to you. Continue that cycle as long as you need, knowing that the Lord is always with you and in you.

In Jesus' name

Do you have to end every prayer with, "in Jesus' name"? Many have been taught that every prayer should end this way. Were you taught that saying "in Jesus' name" would will help to ensure that God would hear your prayers, and hopefully answer? Does ending your prayer requests "in Jesus' name" make you feel better about your lack of confidence in what you just asked God to do? What does "in Jesus' name" really mean?

It is critically important to understand this phrase because Jesus made the most amazing promise to his disciples, and to all believers, on the Thursday night before he was crucified: "*Whatever you ask in my name, this I will do, that the Father may be glorified in the Son. If you ask me anything in my name, I will do it.*" (John 14:13-14) He didn't make this promise just one time that night. He repeated it three more times! (John 14:26, 15:16, 16:23-24) We most definitely need to know what Jesus meant!

Asking in Jesus' name can't be some type of magical formula. It makes no sense at all to think that we can ask for something that is directly opposed to God's will, like coveting, for example, and it be okay because we ended the prayer with the right words. "Father, thank you for bringing to me the new love of my life, the woman I've always dreamed about. My wife no longer understands me. Thank you that this woman does. I know our adultery is wrong, but I thank you for how she makes me feel alive again. Please bless us and help my wife and kids to understand. In Jesus' name." Crazy, right? This example might seem a little extreme but similar prayers happen all too frequently. Not only is this a ridiculous way to pray, it breaks the third of the Ten Commandments by taking the Lord's name in vain. (Exodus 20:7, Deuteronomy 5:11) So how are we to understand what God means when we read phrases about his name or the name of Jesus?

"The name of the LORD" is used frequently in the Old Testament. As just mentioned, it is so important to properly use God's name that he made it the third of the Ten Commandments given to Moses. To understand the meaning, we need to slip our feet into the sandals of the ancient Hebrews. They understood that someone's name represented everything about that person. Children were given names that carried meaning and identity. Moses' name meant, "*I drew him out of the water.*"(Exodus 2:10) When God met with Moses the first time, he told him that his personal name was "Yahweh", which he defined as meaning : "*I AM WHO I AM.*" (Exodus 3:14-15) Both words come from the Hebrew verb "to be". The Hebrews understood that the name of God represented everything about him: what he was like, his nature, his actions, his power, his total being. Psalm 20:6-8 is one of the many references to "the name of the LORD" that helps us understand the significance of the phrase:

Now I know that the LORD saves his anointed;
he will answer him from his holy heaven
with the saving might of his right hand.
Some trust in chariots and some in horses,
but we trust in the name of the LORD our God.
They collapse and fall,
but we rise and stand upright.

It's clear that David was not putting his trust in a word, or in the letters of the name of God. He trusted in God himself to deliver Israel from their enemies. By stating that he was trusting in the name of Yahweh his God, David was emphasizing the trustworthiness of God's character, his power to deliver and his promise to establish David's kingdom. No matter how God chose to rescue them or when he chose to do it, David trusted in his faithful God.

Jews in the New Testament thought similarly about

the phrase "in the name". Here is how the phrase is used in the New Testament: *in the name of the Lord* (twelve times), *in the name of the Lord Jesus* (seven times), *in the name of the Lord Jesus Christ* (once), *in the name of Jesus* (four times), *in the name of Jesus Christ* (four times), *in the name of Jesus Christ of Nazareth* (twice), *in the name of Jesus of Nazareth* (once) and *in the name of Christ* (once). Is there a formula we are to use? Which phrase is the best? Should we alternate using all of them?

There is no magic formula and one phrase is not better than the others. If you go by usage, you could justify that we should end every prayer with: *in the name of the Lord*, since it's used the most frequently. However, if that reasoning were true, it would mean that the other twenty verses were wrong to use the other seven phrases. Of course, this idea is nonsense. Since the Bible is without error, all eight phrases are equally valid in how they call to mind the person of Jesus Christ. That is the key! Each phrase represents the totality of who Jesus is, what he did, all that he is doing and everything that he will do. They depict the essence of his very nature and his will, including all of his plans and desires.

A few verses will help to clarify it further. *But you were washed, you were sanctified, you were justified in the name of the Lord Jesus Christ and by the Spirit of our God.* (1 Corinthians 6:11) All who put their faith in Jesus are washed clean of the guilt of their sinfulness, set apart as holy to God (sanctified) and judged righteous (justified) in the person of Jesus, not in his five letter name (it has five letters in English, but that differs from language to language). We stand forgiven and redeemed in Christ, who suffered for us and rose from the dead. Salvation did not come about when you spoke the two syllable name, "Jesus". Your rescue came about when you entrusted your soul to the

Son of God, to the totality of who he is and all that he did for you. Being in Christ is the same as being forgiven in the name of Christ.

In the beginning weeks of the church in Jerusalem, Peter and John were arrested and ordered by the authorities to stop speaking and teaching *in the name of Jesus* (Acts 4:18). Did the rulers mean that the apostles must not mention that name? That was a small part of it. They were forbidden from teaching people what Jesus did, all of Jesus' teachings and commands and who he really was, which would also include mentioning his very name. Thankfully, the men were empowered by God and absolutely refused the order telling the authorities, to their faces as they were being released: "*for we are unable to stop speaking about what we have seen and heard.*" (Acts 4:20) They had seen the Son of God. They were taught by Emmanuel, which means "God with us". They would give their lives to teach "in the name of Jesus", meaning everything about him and his kingdom.

"In my name"

Yahweh used the phrase in the Old Testament as he warned the people through the prophet Jeremiah not to listen to the false prophets who spoke lies "*in my name*". (Jeremiah 14:14, 15, 23:25, 27:15, 29:9, 29:21, 29:23) The false prophets were wrongly representing God and telling the people what was completely counter to God's Word, his character and his coming judgment. Jesus learned to use this phrase of authority from his Father. He used the same phrase, "in my name", on five different occasions as recorded in Matthew, Mark and Luke. But there is a sixth occasion that stands out from the rest. It was the night of his betrayal. And it was in the context of Jesus teaching his disciples, and all of us followers, about prayer. Here are his statements from that sacred Thursday night recorded in John 14-16:

> "*Whatever you ask in my name, this I will do, that the Father may be glorified in the Son. If you ask me anything in my name, I will do it.*" (14:13-14)
>
> "*But the Helper, the Holy Spirit, whom the Father will send in my name, he will teach you all things and bring to your remembrance all that I have said to you.*" (14:26)
>
> "*You did not choose me, but I chose you and appointed you that you should go and bear fruit and that your fruit should abide, so that whatever you ask the Father in my name, he may give it to you.*" (15:16)
>
> "*In that day you will ask nothing of me. Truly, truly, I say to you, whatever you ask of the Father in my name, he will give it to you.*" (16:23)

All but 14:26 are direct promises from our Lord Jesus that when we ask for something in his name, it will be done. That's amazing! No, that is totally mind-boggling and astounding! But what did Jesus mean? If you and I had the confidence to know how to ask for things in Jesus' name, we would do it much more frequently and with greater assurance. We find Jesus' explanation of what it means to pray in his name here: "*If you abide in me, and my words abide in you, ask whatever you wish, and it will be done for you. By this my Father is glorified, that you bear much fruit and so prove to be my disciples.*" (15:7-8)

To abide in Jesus means to stay with him or remain in him. It means that Jesus truly is the Master of your life; he is the One who you worship and serve. To remain in him means that his words are staying in your heart and head. You are striving to know what Jesus taught and to live by those commands and principles. This is the natural expression of your love for Jesus. If we are following him with our whole hearts, by seeking to live by his words, then and only then can we ask for whatever we want, and the Father will answer. If we are living by the words of Jesus then we are going to ask according to those same words and principles. Our prayer requests will align with what Jesus wants to happen, in us, in those we are praying for, and in our world.

Confidence in our asking doesn't come by ending all of our requests with the phrase "in Jesus' name!" Although, it is good to end some of your prayers this way. Just make sure you understand that this phrase is not some kind of booster rocket that thrusts your requests heavenward. It is equally fine to end your prayers with "Amen". You should also consider closing some of your prayers with a heart-felt, "Thank you" and "I love you", as expressions of your gratitude that you can pray and that the Lord of the universe listens intently. Our confidence in praying comes when we learn how to pray Jesus' way, with his words guiding our requests, so that we are asking the Father for the same things that Jesus himself asks for. What we are really seeking when we pray is for proper alignment with Jesus' life and values. We are asking that our life would be in harmony with his life. We want our devotion to the Father to become like his.

You can always ask him what is on your heart. He wants you to do that. That is, as long as your heart is not directly opposed to God's Word. You may not be certain of God's will in a given situation and you may have a strong desire about how you want things to happen. But we can all learn to pray like Jesus: "*Abba, Father, all things are possible for you. Remove this cup from me. Yet not what I will, but what you will."* The heart God wants to develop in you will pray along with his Son for the Father's will to take precedence over anything that you would like to happen.

Read these powerful words from the old apostle John a few times and let them sink into your heart and soul: *I write these things to you who believe in the name of the Son of God, that you may know that you have eternal life. And this is the confidence that we have toward him, that if we ask anything according to his will he hears us. And if we know that he hears us in whatever we ask, we know that we have the requests that we have asked of him.* (1 John 5:13-15)

The purpose of this book is to help you understand how to keep the words of Jesus abiding in your heart and mind as you pray, so that you will know how to ask God for what he wants to give you. We will explore how to know God's will so that you can ask accordingly. But there is one more truth to consider before we dive in.

Direct access

One of the most astounding truths in rescuing his people from sin, death and hell is that we now have direct access to the Father. In Christ, direct access is a radically new concept. God visibly demonstrated to the Jews, through how the temple was arranged, that his holiness was unapproachable for humans. You may know that there was one room in the Temple, the Most Holy Place, where God's presence was always visible. By day there was a plume of smoke that hovered over this room and towered up into the sky. By night it was a column of fire. In God's law, he gave the command that only one person could ever enter this room and that was the High Priest. However, he couldn't go in whenever he wanted; he could only enter one day each year for a very specific reason. This day was called Yom Kippur, which means The Day of Atonement. In 1 Timothy 6:15b-16, we read this same truth, that God is *the blessed and only Sovereign, the King of kings and Lord of lords, who alone is immortality, who dwells in unapproachable light, whom no one has ever seen or can see.*

On the Day of Atonement the High Priest would symbolically make atonement for all of Israel's sins through a blood sacrifice. Since the time of Moses, the Jews celebrated this momentous day. Jewish tradition says that the Jews were so fearful of entering into this room where God dwelt, that they tied a rope around the High Priest's ankle so that if he did something wrong and God struck him dead, they could drag his body from the room. They knew that if anyone else entered the Most Holy Place to retrieve the body, they too would be struck dead by God. That might sound harsh, but God was demonstrating the truth that he is completely holy and thus lives in unapproachable light. That is his holiness. The purpose of the Day of Atonement was to point to the day when God would atone for the sins of his people through the blood sacrifice of his Lamb, the Lord Jesus Christ.

The power of Jesus' sacrificial death was demonstrated in a very visible way to the Jews when Jesus breathed his last breath on that sacred Friday afternoon. *And Jesus cried out again with a loud voice and yielded up his spirit. And behold, the curtain of the temple was torn in two, from top to bottom. And the earth shook, and the rocks were split.* (Matthew 27:50-51) The gigantic curtain that served as the door into the Most Holy Place was now opened up for anyone to enter! God demonstrated to the world that through his Son's sacrifice, people could now have access into his presence, but only through accepting that Jesus is the Lamb of God that atones for the sins of those who believe.

In Hebrews 10:19-22, this astonishing new reality is described: *Therefore, brothers, since we have confidence to enter the holy places by the blood of Jesus, by the new and living way that he opened for us through the curtain, that is, through his flesh, and since we have a great priest over the house of God, let us draw near with a true heart in full assurance of faith, with our hearts sprinkled clean from an evil conscience and our bodies washed with pure water.*

We get to draw near to God! In Christ, we can have absolute confidence, even though we can't see him, that we are praying directly to God and he is listening to our every word. Our confidence is in Jesus. Only sinless people can stand to be in God's presence. You and I certainly are far from being sinless, practically speaking, but we most definitely are sinless *positionally*. Jesus has atoned for all of our sins and we therefore stand before his Father and ours, covered in Jesus' righteousness, in his holiness. Have full assurance that when you pray, you are speaking to your heavenly Father, just as if you are standing right in front of him. Not quibbling and terrified like Dorothy and her friends were when they stood before the powerful Oz. Rather, it's like a dearly loved child sitting on his father's lap because he adores and trusts him so completely.

Another amazing truth is that our prayers are not lost in space. God not only hears us, he also captures our requests, confessions and praises. Here is the indelible picture from Revelation 5:8: *And when he had taken the scroll* (Jesus), *the four living creatures and the twenty-four elders fell down before the Lamb, each holding a harp, and golden bowls full of incense, which are the prayers of the saints.* Our prayers are forever captured in golden bowls of incense; our prayers are a sweet aroma in the Father's nostrils. Revelation 8:3-4 give the same image. What a picture! Shouldn't that reinforce our desire to want to pray according to the will of God? If our prayers are that precious to the Father, we can strive to do better, much better. We can learn to pray in truer alignment with how God wants us to pray, using his way and his words. How could you possibly go wrong praying to the Father according to the pattern that his Son gave to us?

The Followers' Prayer

Luke 11:2-4 and Matthew 6:9-13 are usually referred to as "the Lord's Prayer". But is this what Jesus actually prayed? Did he intend for us to memorize these very words and recite them as we pray? No. This is not the Lord's prayer but "The Followers' Prayer". Jesus gave us a very detailed outline, or framework, for how we are to ask God for the things he wants to give us. It's the pattern for all of us as the people of his kingdom, for talking with our heavenly Father about all the things that concern both us and him. This outline is how we develop a powerful habit of engaging in rich, meaningful conversations with the God of the universe.

In the next chapter, we'll discover how to use this outline of praying in order to better understand how to ask the Father for what he wants to give us. But let's be perfectly clear: we are not learning how to manipulate God to get what we want. Praying the way God wants you to pray isn't the end goal. Our praying is all about developing an intimate relationship with our Father, his Son and the Holy Spirit. Seeing God answer our prayers is about building up our faith in him as we watch him work in and through us to bring about his kingdom in a broken and dark world.

The way to love the Lord with all your heart, soul, mind and strength is completely dependent on learning how to converse with him regularly, as you think like Jesus while praying. Never forget that what Jesus told his disciples on that Thursday night, he also spoke to you and me; "*No longer do I call you servants, for the servant does not know what his master is doing; but I have called you friends, for all that I have heard from my* Father, *I have made known to you.*" (John 15:15)

Small Group Questions

1. What keeps you from praying more frequently? What do you think a good remedy might be for you?

2. Have you prayed for something for a long time? How did God answer your request? What did you learn during the process?

3. Discuss what stands out to you the most in Luke 11:1-13. Compare and contrast the story of the friend with the analogy of the father and Jesus' promise of v13. How might these truths impact your praying?

4. How is the Spirit all that you need? Discuss a current situation in your life and determine how the Spirit is the answer to that situation.

5. How do you understand what Jesus meant about praying in his name? What does it not mean? Why does it matter how you begin and end your prayers?

CHAPTER 2 - THE FOLLOWERS' PRAYER

"Father, hallowed be your name.
Your kingdom come.
Give us each day our daily bread,
and forgive us our sins,
for we ourselves forgive everyone who is indebted to us.
And lead us not into temptation."

Kids really do say the darndest things. They listen to how their parents, older siblings, grandparents and pastors pray. They then try to mimic what they hear. One little boy, when asked to pray, began with great confidence, "Our Father, who does art in heaven, Harold is his name." A four-year-old stated boldly, "and forgive us our trash baskets as we forgive those who put trash in our baskets." His thinking isn't too far from the truth. At just three years old, Caitlin closed her prayer stating, "and lead us not into temptation, but deliver us from email." Wouldn't it better to teach children how to think as they pray rather than just recite words?

Did Jesus mean the words above are what we should

actually speak when we pray? There are only 36 words in this translation from the *English Standard Version.* In the original Greek, there are 38 words. Reciting it at a normal pace will take you between 13-15 seconds. Was Jesus purpose to give us a prayer we could recite in 13-15 seconds? Was that his answer to his disciples request to teach them how to pray? Is he giving us just a few words to say because we are such busy people? Not a chance.

Of course Jesus dialogued with his Father about everything. He would often get away from his disciples to spend personal time with his Father, uninterrupted by the world. Sometimes he would pray for hours, even through the night. In the prayer outline, Jesus is teaching us how to have the same kinds of intimate conversations with the Father as he was accustomed to having. Therefore, he gave us an outline of how to arrange our prayers. This outline is the framework we build upon as we learn to more freely talk with our Father in the heavens throughout the day about everything that concerns us and him.

We are not free to ask him for anything we want, however. Imagine if you gave your child or a friend everything they ever asked of you? Jesus knows us intimately and knows that if we are left on our own, we'll ask for things that may actually be bad for us or even hurt others. Our human nature is all about self at the core, so without proper guidance from Jesus, and the Spirit's help too, we'll end up asking for whatever works best for us, and only us. We're all very good at praying according to the Me Monster within.

So how do we build our confidence that we really do know what to ask of God? How do we reject the incessant desires of the Me Monster? You don't have to figure it out on your own. You don't have to wonder if you got it right. Jesus' words are like your Maps app, guiding you where you need to go. We must center our lives, and most definitely our conversations with God, on Jesus' teaching of how he instructed us to *order* our praying.

The apostle John had over 60 years of living in an intimate relationship with the Father when he was led by the Spirit to write in 1 John 5:14-15: *This is the confidence we have toward him, that if we ask anything according to his will he hears us. And if we know that he hears us in whatever we ask, we know that we have the requests that we have asked of him.* We considered this passage in Chapter 1.

The closer our requests align with God's will, the more we can expect to receive what we ask for. How do we know his will? That's the ten million dollar question, isn't it? You, like me, want to know God's will for your life in all kinds of situations. Should I take this job? Should we move? Should I date this person? On and on our questions go, wondering what God's will for us really is.

His will is in black and white. He gave us his will in his words. It's written down for you and it has been protected for over 2,000 years. There is no other piece of literature that can be compared to the Bible in reliability. There are so many ancient copies of manuscripts of the Bible in existence that we can know for certain it is God's revealed message to humanity. We have it in more English translations that any of us will ever read. You have it right before you. God has already spoken to us about how to ask him, according to his will, through his Word who became flesh, Jesus. The key to asking God with confidence is asking according to his holy Word, which obviously is his perfect will. Is he the kind of God who would withhold critical information that we need?

The prayer outline is our guide to praying according to the will of God. "But I want specifics about his will!", you might be thinking. So do I. The specific answers you need will come through the Spirit as you pray according to this outline given to us by the Son of God. So let's dive in.

1st "Father, hallowed be your name."

Every conversation we have is dependent upon the person we're speaking with. Naturally, Jesus taught us to address God as our Father who is holy. To call the Almighty Creator and Sustainer of the cosmos, "our Father", is a mind-boggling privilege. We have the right to call him our Father because he chose to adopt us into his holy family. (Romans 8:15) Our union with Christ that makes us sons and daughters through faith is so binding that we also have the incredible privilege to call him "Abba".

Abba was the common Aramaic term of endearment that a child would call his father. In Jesus' day, the people in Israel spoke mostly in Aramaic and they wrote in Greek. The term also captures the sense of deep respect for a father. Was there a time when you wrote a card or addressed your dad with deep love, gratitude and respect? How did you address him? Was it, "Dear Dad", or something similar? This is the idea with the ancient word "Abba". It carried with it a deep and trusting love along with an unwavering respect and admiration.

Jesus taught his followers to begin their prayer by acknowledging their new relationship to God. Calling the God of their forefathers "Father" was a new concept for these Jewish people. It likely seemed much too informal to them initially. We've been using the term so long now that it has become common place for us. However, reflecting on passages like Ephesians 1:3-14 can remind us of the high privilege we have been given through Christ to be able to call the God of all creation, our Father.

Focusing on the reality of why you can call him your Father in the heavens will greatly impact how you pray. You may begin with thoughts like: "Thank you, heavenly Father, for showing me who Jesus is and for giving me the faith to believe that you gave him to us to suffer, die and rise again. Thank you that in him I have a brand new life, both on this earth and in the next life with you. I praise you that you are my Father who loves me with an endless love. I believe that nothing in the seen world or unseen world can separate me from your love. You are an amazing Father, full of love and patience for me and for all who trust in your Son. Thank you, Father, for giving me your grace when I don't even recognize what you have done. Thank you, Father, that all of your promises to me are certain and all of your words are true. Help me now to speak with you in a way that honors you and pleases you and makes you smile."

Imagine how much pleasure your heavenly Father finds in hearing you say things like that. Once you get used to spending time thanking God that you are his son or daughter, thoughts about your high privilege of being part of his family will flow much more easily and naturally. This is the idea behind *hallowed be your name*. We not only need to address God properly as our Father, we must thank him for the kind of Father he is. Consequently, we want everyone we know and love to also recognize God's holiness. Jesus said that the Spirit would come in the world to convince people of their sin and God's holiness.

In Jesus' day, to use the word "name" meant to refer to everything about the person. The "name" includes the person's character, their reputation, all that they are and all that they do. Stating that our Father's name is holy means we are recognizing that everything about God is completely pure and set apart. All that he is and does is holy and there is nothing about him that isn't holy. His holiness means that he isn't like us at all. Isn't that good news? You wouldn't want God to be like you, would you? God's holiness encapsulates all of his other qualities like his love, patience, kindness, goodness, faithfulness, persistence, dependability and truthfulness. In the prayer outline, we begin by acknowledging who he is and what he is like.

The Psalms are full of beautiful addresses to God that capture poetically how Jesus taught us to begin our prayers. One such example is Psalm 103:1-5;

Bless the LORD, O my soul,
and all that is within me,
bless his holy name!
Bless the LORD, O my soul,
and forget not all his benefits,
who forgives all your iniquity,
who heals all your diseases,
who redeems your life from the pit,
who crowns you with steadfast love and mercy,
who satisfies you with good
so that your youth is renewed like the eagle's.

Each time you see his name written in the Bible with small caps, LORD, be reminded just how holy he is. In Exodus 3:14-15, God, the Maker of heaven and earth, told Moses that his personal name is Yhwh. From the Hebrew language, we only know these 4 consonants and we're not certain of the vowels. The Jewish people considered this personal name of God to be so holy that they would not pronounce it, so we have lost the exact spelling. Therefore, they would pronounce the word Yhwh as Adonay, which means "Lord". When the vowels of Adonay are placed with Yhwh, the name becomes "Jehovah". In recent years, many theologians have come to believe the more proper way to refer to the personal name of God is with the name, "Yahweh". Jews who saw his presence manifested before them on Mount Sinai understood the magnitude of his holiness, which instilled within them the fear to even pronounce his personal name. They missed the whole point of God's holiness. He revealed himself to them so that they could know him personally and call him by his personal name, Yahweh. Yahweh is God's covenant name. Therefore, each time you see "LORD" as you read the Bible, remember that his name is Yahweh and that you have been given the privilege to call him Father. Jesus taught us that his Father is now our Father because we have been adopted into the holy family. We are all, through faith in Jesus Christ, sons and daughters of the Most High King. That is amazing and something we need to focus on more and more, each and every day.

It may be helpful as you begin to pray to picture the scene in Isaiah 6:1-7 when Isaiah was taken up into heaven. He saw the Lord seated on a throne with seraphim circling above him calling out; "*Holy, holy, holy is the LORD of hosts; the whole earth is full of his glory.*" Immediately the prophet is seized with the reality of Yahweh's holiness and his own personal sinfulness. I find it helpful to declare with the seraphim this majestic declaration of Yahweh. He is before all things and in him all things hold together. Let us be quick to acknowledge that we are beginning to understand how marvelous and full of splendor he actually is. As you remind your soul who God is and what he is like, your problems will quickly diminish and your perspective about life will take on new hope. As you concentrate on who you are praying to, it will impact what you say and what you think. You will be less likely to fall asleep or get side tracked with competing thoughts. It may help you to think of a favorite story that depicts God's character or picture a scene from nature that declares God's holiness. Find what works for you to remain focused on your conversation with God the Almighty who loves to listen to your prayers.

2nd "Your kingdom come."

Jesus' teaching about prayer in Luke 11 came approximately 2 years after his sermon on the hill in Matthew 5-7. In that teaching, he included the phrase, *your will be done on earth as it is in heaven*, to the request about God's kingdom coming. This is the most unfamiliar part of the prayer and one we must spend more time on to fully understand how to pray God's will.

How do things happen in heaven? God is always fully obeyed. The angels and all the saints who have gone before us are all there, in absolute paradise in the presence of the Father and the Son. Everyone basks in the love of God and in the power of the Almighty. There is no sin, no sorrow, no injustice, no pain, no loneliness or hopelessness. There is only joy and absolute fulfillment and purpose in the presence of Yahweh. It is so breathtakingly astonishing that when the apostle Paul was taken up into heaven he wrote that he heard *things that cannot be told, which man may not utter.* (2 Corinthians

12:4) The splendor and majesty of the visible presence of God will eclipse every bad experience and memory we ever had on earth.

Jesus' favorite topic to teach about was the fact that the kingdom of God had come to earth, because the King of heaven was standing before them. Emmanuel, which means God with us, was indeed with them! The rule and reign of God was now on the earth and the end of sin, death and hell was certain.

The Spirit inspired Matthew to use the phrase "the kingdom of heaven" while Mark and Luke were led to write "the kingdom of God". The phrases are obviously synonymous. Jesus came teaching about the kingdom because the kingdom of God is everything. After his resurrection, Luke's second letter to Theophilus states this: *He presented himself alive to them after his suffering by many proofs, appearing to them during forty days and speaking about the kingdom of God.* (Acts 1:3) What is the Kingdom?

Jesus taught us to ask that our lives align with life in the Kingdom. It is a very sweeping request ranging from the ending of all injustice to his followers living in full obedience and unwavering devotion. Of course the prayer also means that people everywhere will come to faith in Jesus and become sons and daughters of Yahweh. As the Kingdom comes in our lives and homes and communities, everything must change. Just as Jesus taught in Matthew 6, it's about everything happening on earth like in heaven.

When Jesus summed up what obedience to his Father looks like, he helped us picture what the kingdom of heaven does when it comes into a life: "*You shall love the Lord your God with all your heart and with all your soul and with all your strength and with all your mind, and your neighbor as yourself.*" Well that's easy, right?

No! That kind of transformed life only happens as we engage with our Father in the heavens by asking him to make those changes happen within us. Instead of wanting our daily bread, we are to long for our hearts and minds to be transformed so that we think and act more and more like Jesus.

Because this kind of request is so foreign to our human nature, so challenging to maintain and so misunderstood and underutilized, I will take the rest of this book to demonstrate from the Bible exactly what "Kingdom Come Praying" involves. This is the kind of praying that we must learn because it does not come to us naturally. It comes super-naturally or a better term is "Spirit-naturally". To live our lives as kingdom people we must be radically dependent on the Spirit of Christ to work in us and through us. The potential for each of us to become like the kind of person Jesus was is astounding. It is God's will. That is why I will take the remaining chapters to explore "Kingdom Come Praying" so that you can begin to center these kinds of requests into your regular conversations with the Father.

Don't miss the order of Jesus' outline for our praying. It begins with acknowledging who God is and what he is like. He then tells us to talk to our Father about the most important aspects of our lives, how we align with the Kingdom – our spiritual transformation by the indwelling Spirit of God.

3rd "Give us each day our daily bread,"

The next category of requests that Jesus gave us is to ask God to: *Give us each day our daily bread.* The Greek phrase could also be translated *our bread for tomorrow.* Jesus gave us the freedom to ask our Father for the things that we need in life. For his audience, food was the most pressing need. But that's not true for most of us and for many followers of Jesus around the world, and yet it still is for some. Therefore, Jesus opened the door for us to ask his Father for those things that we need in life, just like the man who had the midnight caller.

As I write this, we're a few weeks from closing on our home and moving to another city. If you've ever sold a home, you know all those anxious moments that come before the actual closing. We had one yesterday. The termite inspector told us he found evidence of some of the little varmints on one of the foundation pillars, but not in the flooring. "What?! Our home isn't even 5 years old and it was pretreated at construction. We can't have termites!" To make matters worse, he stated that the treatment would run around $1,000. It was one of those kick-in-the-gut moments that robs our joy and replaces it with anxiety.

We all have needs. Sometimes those needs are so heavy on us that we can barely function. Whether they are about health, finances, relationships (or the lack thereof), legal matters or emotional issues, we all have needs. Have you noticed that it is those tangible needs that usually dominate your praying? When prayers are offered in a church setting or small group, what kinds of things are typically requested? Isn't it almost always about the tangible things that people need – health, safety or money? In many of the meetings I've participated in over the years, much more time is often spent talking about those needs and all the challenging circumstances rather than actually praying for the person.

Isn't this why Jesus instructed us to pray about kingdom things *before* we pray about our physical and relational needs? The order of the outline is critically important if we're going to develop our conversations with the Father to the depth that he desires. Jesus' brilliance is on display again in the order of our requests. As you pray first for spiritual transformation, it will greatly impact your perspective on the tangible things in your life. As you think about the kingdom coming in your life or the person you are praying for, it will have a profound impact on how you see tangible needs. Praying for someone's health takes on an entirely new perspective when you begin praying for them by asking God to give them his Spirit, flooding their heart with the light of his Word or strengthening them to be able to endure the illness with the joy of the Lord.

The wonderful news is that Jesus did include this category of physical needs in "The Followers' Prayer". He cares deeply about us, so he also cares about our needs. Don't forget the stories of the midnight traveler and the old widow. Jesus knows from his own experience of living as a human how important food, shelter and clothing is to us. That's why in his long sermon on the hill, he talked specifically about our needs and how to conquer anxiety.

Matthew recorded the sermon in chapters 5-7. The portion that addresses the necessities of life is found in 6:25-34. This is a wonderful passage to mediate through anytime you feel overwhelmed with life's circumstances. Referring to the things we need to live, Jesus assured us that, "*your heavenly Father knows that you need them all.*" Notice that Jesus added the word "all". Isn't it comforting to realize that the Father knows absolutely every detail about your life and everything you need? Jesus is teaching us how incredibly valuable we are to his Father and since he knows everything about us and all that we truly need, he will provide accordingly. That doesn't mean we'll receive all of our wants, but our needs are covered. I have found that the more I asked and sought and knocked, many of my wants would simply go away. I have often lost the desire for something that I thought I really needed by continuing to talk to my Father about that which I wanted to happen or not happen.

In that sermon on the hill, Jesus instructed his listeners, and all of us since that day: "*Therefore, do not be anxious, saying, 'What shall we eat?' or 'What shall we drink?' or 'What shall we wear?'* Why should the people of God not be anxious about the necessities of life? Isn't that simply part of the human experience? Jesus gave the answer. We don't have to worry because God knows we need these things. We must trust him that everything will work out for the good to everyone who loves Jesus, just like he promised in Romans 8:28. Overcoming anxiety is a matter of faith. And faith is put to work through our praying to God about those things that make us anxious.

Let's take a look at the passage I referenced in the previous chapter. *Rejoice in the Lord always; again I will say, rejoice. Let your reasonableness be known to everyone. The Lord is at hand; do not be anxious about anything, but in everything by prayer and supplication with thanksgiving let your requests be made known to God. And the peace of God, which surpasses all understanding, will guard your hearts and your minds in Christ Jesus.* (Philippians 4:4-7)

Our outline for praying is firmly embedded in this most wonderful passage. Before dealing with our anxiety, the Spirit reminds us that he is near, he is present, just like the opening category of the prayer: *Our* Father. That God hears us means that he is present with us. He is always with us and can never abandon us or get so busy that he forgets to check on us. We live in the presence of the Most High God through the Holy Spirit who inhabits us 24/7. When Jesus said that he would never leave his followers or forget about them, he meant it. His presence is always with us through his Spirit. The Father, the Son and the Spirit are in absolute unity.

Because we're thinking about the reality of the Holy Spirit living with us, we need not succumb to the effects of being anxious and worried. How do you tend to act when you're worried. Aren't you more irritable? You don't have the patience or kindness you normally have. Worry can greatly impact your mood and that's why the verse tells us to let others see our "reasonableness". The original word also conveys the idea of having a gentle and patient spirit. Instead of being ill with others when you're dealing with things that cause worry, you can be gracious with them. You don't have to let worry, stress or anxiety ruin your mood or your day or someone else's day because you were mean to them.

The peace of God guards our thinking and our emotions as we talk to our Father about everything that causes worry. So the Word tells us: *do not be anxious about anything, but in everything* tell God all of your requests through all kinds of praying. The way to conquer anxiety and worry is to talk about your needs with your Holy Father.

If the worry returns, talk about it again with your Father until you sense his peace replacing the worry and fear. Live in that peace until the worry returns and simply take it up again with your Father in the heavens who loves to hear you call out to him. If it's really important to you, then you must talk to your Father about it. It's not so he'll know, but so you'll know you've told him. We get honest with ourselves as we speak openly with God about everything. This is Jesus' teaching to us because it is exactly how he lived his life while sojourning on this earth.

Are there things in your life about which you don't feel comfortable asking God for his help? Why is that? Do you think you need to take care of the small stuff by yourself? Is it something you would rather just handle on your own? It might be helpful to spend some time working through these questions. Why don't you ask God for his help in the not-so-critical situations in your life?

You can practice your dependence on God by talking to him more frequently about all the things you want and need. If you're in a hurry and can't find the keys, stop and ask your Father to help you find them. Begin praying to him about the little things and that may well help you with life's larger issues.

Not flare prayers

Flare prayers are those times when we're in the heat of the battle and need immediate help from our Father through his Spirit. Flare prayers are very powerful and frequently needed. When you're losing your cool in traffic, you need a flare prayer. "God, help me chill and get my head screwed back on!" Flare prayers are needed when you receive an email, text or post that puts you in a sudden rage. "Father, please empower me now with your strength and peace to not react like I want to react, but like you want me to!" "Father, my husband did it again! Help me to control my temper." Those are the kinds of flare prayers that we need to be launching up to God throughout the day.

The Followers' Prayer is an outline for when you're ready to take some time to have a significant conversation with God. To work through the outline that Jesus gave us can't be done in a couple of minutes. It's certainly not a flare prayer. Remember that Jesus gave the outline in a specific context. His disciples had been watching him pray and they asked him to teach them how to pray. From the context, we know that our Lord was teaching his followers how to spend quality time asking, seeking and knocking.

I suggest that if you aren't in the habit of praying 15-30 minutes in one sitting, begin with 10 minutes. Discipline yourself to go to a quiet place with the outline in hand and begin to work through it. You will find that the time passes very quickly. As you build this type of praying into your daily routine, you will find it easy to increase the amount of time you spend. At one time, I had a 45 minute commute to work. I often used that commute time, or part of it, to talk to my Father in the heavens. The goal is not to focus on the amount of time you are praying. The goal is to strengthen your relationship with God as you grow in your dependence on him. Let's continue with the prayer outline.

4th "and forgive us our sins..."

For most of us, acknowledging our failures to our Father is a part of prayer that's neglected. Jesus taught us that we're to keep very short accounts with God. Is it that we need to tell him the bad we've done and the good we've failed to do?

The power of confessing your sins to God can't be overemphasized. Can you remember when you were a child and had to confess your guilt to your parents? Can you remember how you felt before you confessed? Do you remember how the guilt made you feel terrible. Confessing that you were the one responsible set you free to experience the discipline you deserved. You didn't want the spanking or being imprisoned in your room, but it was worth it just to be free from the guilt.

You need to confess all of your sins specifically in order to gain victory over them. You can't begin to conquer a short temper until you acknowledge that you have a short temper. Jealousy will continue to dog you until you begin to confess to your Father every time you feel jealous. That's just the way life works in the Kingdom.

Confessing is the reality of looking within your heart and acknowledging the truth about how you act and feel. It's the act of coming clean with God and accepting the ugliness in you that he wants to help you overcome. So ask yourself a soul-penetrating question: Why don't I confess my sins to God more frequently and more specifically?

Jesus added this part to our prayer outline because he knows how beneficial it will be for every one of his followers. He also knows that a powerful way to minimize pride and over-confidence in ourselves is to regularly tell the Father how we've messed up. And don't ever forget that we need to confess both kinds of sin – omission and commission. We usually know when we've done wrong. Those are sins of commission. Equally sinful to God, though, are the times when we fail to do what's right. We fail to love, forgive, encourage or serve someone in the realm of our influence. Those are sins of omission. It's critically important to confess all sins.

The temptation in this area of prayer is to use a wide brush stroke and generalize our failures. "God, forgive me for coveting." Do you think that's what your heavenly Father wants to hear? Did your parent want to hear, "Mommy, forgive me for disobeying you."? Or did she want to hear you say, "Forgive me for not cleaning up my room like you asked me to do." You get the point.

Let's consider again the words of the old apostle John. *If we say we have no sin, we deceive ourselves, and the truth is not in us. If we confess our sins, he is faithful and just to forgive us our sins and to cleanse us from all unrighteousness.* (1 John 1:8-9)

Remember, he wrote his letters when he was a very old man, probably 30 years after all the other letters of the New Testament had been written and circulated. John knew personally the power of confessing his sins and how it cleansed his soul from the pain of personal guilt. John is writing about our personal relationship with the Father and how not confessing our sins hinders that intimacy. We all know this reality and have likely experienced it many times in our personal relationships. Everyone who is married definitely knows how personal hurts fractures the marriage relationship.

Our temptation is that we get slack or lazy or just too busy. We don't really want to think about all of our failures so we tend not to bring it up when we're praying. Jesus is reminding us that we must take the time to keep a clean heart before our Father who knows all our secrets, so why even try to keep secrets from him?

Who owes you?

The most powerful reality of confessing your sins regularly to God is how it will change your perspective towards others. The sins that they commit against you will diminish the more you honestly acknowledge your sins against God. Stop and underline that sentence. Read it a few more times and let that truth sink in. It is true. As you look within and acknowledge all of your sins against the Father your perspective will be changed.

Think of someone who has wronged you. What did they do or not do? How did it make you feel? Are you having trouble forgiving them, either in your heart or to them personally? Now ask yourself how many times have you committed a similar sin against God. You simply have no reason why you can't forgive the other person's sin against you. None!

Jesus was obviously very intentional with his words. He told us to confess our sins, using the normal word for sins, *harmartia.* It literally means to miss the mark and is the typical word used for all sins against God. Did you catch the word Jesus used to describe when we forgive others? Debts. Jesus taught us to pray and ask the Father to forgive our sins in the same way that we forgive everyone "*who is indebted to us*". The word means to owe money, unless it's used as a metaphor, like Jesus used it here.

Who owes you something? I can think of lots of people who I believe owe me an apology, some owe me a response (email, text or call), others owe me more respect and still others owe me their gratitude. What do people owe you? How big is their indebtedness? These debts are real and hurtful. People really do owe us. But are we entitled to collect, ever?

Peter asked Jesus how often he should forgive his brother who sinned against him. The standard answer in those days was seven. But Jesus answered Peter by telling him he should forgive his brother "*seventy-sevens*". Jesus didn't mean Peter needed to keep count until he reached 490. Jesus meant that forgiveness is without limits. Then he told one of the most profound parables that you'll ever read.

A story of debts owed

"Therefore the kingdom of heaven may be compared to a king who wished to settle accounts with his servants. When he began to settle, one was brought to him who owed him ten thousand talents. And since he could not pay, his master ordered him to be sold, with his wife and children and all that he had, and payment to be made. So the servant fell on his knees, imploring him, 'Have patience with me, and I will pay you everything.' And out of pity for him, the master of that servant released him and forgave him the debt. But when that same servant went out, he found one of his fellow servants who owed him a hundred denarii, and seizing him, he began to choke him, saying, 'Pay what you owe.' So his fellow servant fell down and pleaded with him, 'Have patience with me, and I will pay you.' He refused and went and put him in prison until he should pay the debt. When his fellow servants saw what had taken place, they were greatly distressed, and they went and reported to their master all that had taken place. Then his master summoned him and said to him, 'You wicked servant! I forgave you all that debt because you pleaded with me. And should not you have had mercy on your fellow servant, as I had mercy on you?' And in anger his master delivered him to the jailers, until he should pay all his debt. So also my heavenly Father will do to every one of you, if you do not forgive your brother from your heart." (Matthew 18:23-35)

We must dig into Jesus' words to understand the power of this story. A "talent" was a huge amount of money that was worth approximately 20 years of a typical laborer's wages. The servant owed the king an absolutely mind boggling amount of money. It would have been impossible for Jesus' disciples to have been able to wrap their minds around that large of a debt. Taking the current average annual salary of a worker in the U.S., the equivalent amount owed today is over $16 billion!

The king forgave his servant a debt of $16 billion dollars because he had pity on the man. Yes, the servant vowed to repay the king, but they both knew full well that repayment was absolutely impossible.

When the servant is released from the debt, he apparently went straight to another servant who owed him money and demanded repayment. That debt was a hundred denarii. A denarius was a day's wage. So the equivalent for us today is about $20 thousand. That's a lot of money. If someone owes you $20 grand, you're definitely going to do all you can to collect it, just like the servant in the story. But not if you've just been forgiven a debt of over $16 billion. The comparative ratio is 800,000 to 1!

Maybe someone has done something really bad to you and if you could put it into dollars, it might be worth $20 thousand. Maybe they ruined your reputation or cheated on you or stole from you. No matter the crime, Jesus tells us to forgive and keep forgiving. There is no limit to us forgiving others.

What's the basis? God has forgiven you of your astronomical debt! It was a debt that you had no chance of ever repaying, or even making a dent in. What you owed God was so beyond your ability to repay that the only way for you to be forgiven was through his mercy. Without question, God expects all who have received his immeasurable mercy to extend a similar mercy to everyone else. Now go back and read how Jesus ended the story.

Could he have been any clearer? Is there any question

about God's expectation of you? And the forgiveness you extend to others is to come directly "*from your heart*".

As you look into your own heart and consider the past 24 hours, you will discover how you have failed God. But you don't have to wallow in your guilt and remorse. Confess each time you failed him, even if it's the same sin you keep repeating every day. Confess and believe that your relationship with the Father is fully restored, if you have also forgiven the record of debts owed to you.

It's hard work. It takes deep honesty to admit you have not truly forgiven someone. But you can do it, with God's help. And as you pray and confess your sins, don't hesitate to ask his help to strengthen you to forgive all of those who owe you. You may need to read this story frequently or memorize the 800,000 : 1 ratio. I find it helpful to think about my life and how our Father has forgiven me of so many things. I recall how he keeps forgiving me of the sins that I keep repeating, over and over again. My Father never grows weary of hearing me confess my continual faults to him because that's when he can help me the most to eventually overcome and conquer those temptations.

Realize that those who you must forgive probably don't deserve it. In Jesus' story, neither servant deserved forgiveness, and neither do you. We can only forgive others on the basis of God's forgiveness. You give someone mercy because God has given you mercy. Your forgiveness isn't so much about your relationship with that other person as it is about your relationship with God. Forgive them because Jesus wants you to forgive them. Wipe away their debt to you because this gives your Father in the heavens great pleasure.

The apostle Paul was inspired to write these words: *Put on then, as God's chosen ones, holy and beloved, compassionate hearts, kindness, humility, meekness, and patience, bearing with one another and, if one has a complaint against another, forgiving each other; as the Lord has forgiven you, so you also must forgive.* (Colossians 3:12-13)

Our human nature gets all twisted up wanting justice. We want people to get what they deserve. We will not be a door mat and let others walk all over us. Those are the attitudes of the Me Monster within, for all of us.

Forgiveness comes as we turn our focus on God and how he doesn't give us what we deserve. He gives us mercy and grace and we are commanded to do the same. In Christ, you've received $16 billion in mercy and grace to your account. There's plenty there to give out to everyone who owes you a little something. Confess and forgive.

5th "And lead us not into temptation."

We're now on the fifth and final part of the outline of The Followers' Prayer. Jesus gave us the directive to ask his Father to lead us out of every temptation. The language is a little confusing for us. The way Jesus phrased it, it sounds like God might very well lead us into temptations that can take us down. Did this last part of the prayer confuse you when you learned to recite it? Do you remember hearing the prayer recited in church, not knowing how this leading worked? We must understand exactly what Jesus meant by this last request.

James, one of Jesus' half-brothers, helps us to understand what we already sense in our hearts – that God doesn't tempt us to sin. *Blessed is the man who remains steadfast under trial, for when he has stood the test he will receive the crown of life, which God has promised to those who love him. Let no one say when he is tempted, "I am being tempted by God," for God cannot be tempted with evil, and he himself tempts no one.*

But each person is tempted when he is lured and enticed by his own desire. Then desire when it has conceived gives birth to sin, and sin when it is fully grown brings forth death. (James 1:12-15)

Where do temptations come from? Temptations to sin are all around us in society, they come from the Me Monster within us and from Satan and his evil domain. Jesus gave us a rhetorical statement that carries great force when we understand correctly how to successfully navigate the countless landmines of temptations.

We understand the origins of temptations and how to overcome them from a classic passage in 1 Corinthians 10:1-13. Many followers of Jesus have memorized v13 (next paragraph). In this passage, the apostle Paul reminds us that God preserved the Hebrew scriptures, the Old Testament, in order to give us instruction, reveal to us his ways and to give us examples of how to live and not live. His point in the first twelve verses is that we all must be very careful with our lives and do all that we can to follow closely after God and avoid sinning as much as possible. Sin always has consequences. Sometimes those consequences are catastrophic, sometimes they are not so great. But all sin is rebellion against God and it always costs something. So our best choice is don't sin. But we all fail at times. How can we improve?

Here is that powerful verse; *No temptation has overtaken you that is not common to man. God is faithful, and he will not let you be tempted beyond your ability, but with the temptation he will also provide a way of escape, that you may be able to endure it.* What an encouraging truth. We don't have to sin!

How can God keep us from being tempted beyond our ability as well as give us a way of escape if he is not present with us? That is at the core of this truth. God is with us. The Psalmist wrote: *God is our refuge and strength, a very present help in trouble.* (Psalm 46:1) Jesus promised to everyone who trusts in him that he would never leave them or forget about them. The Father and the Son are actually present with us every moment of every day through the Spirit who lives within us.

You face all kinds of temptations to sin. Anger, pride, lack of love, coveting, jealousy, bickering, unforgiveness and sexual immorality are all common temptations. That's what the Bible reminds us. We all face the same kinds of temptations. They are common to everyone, but we need not give in to all or any of those temptations because God is always faithful to us. He knows what we can handle and what we can't. He is well aware of your strengths and all of your weaknesses. He will challenge you to grow in your dependence on him, but he does not want you to fail him. He wants you to overcome every temptation and he always provides a way of escaping each temptation.

Isn't it comforting to know that God has such intimate knowledge of you that he knows where you're vulnerable? He knows when you get angry in traffic, are tempted to view porn on the web or feel jealousy towards your co-worker. God's plan for your life is for you to lean on him at all times, especially when you are being tempted. In the next chapters of this book, we will discover much more about *the way of escape* that he provides. But for now, be assured that you can overcome any temptation by turning to him for help.

This is why Jesus ended our prayer outline by having us ask God to show us the way of escape throughout each day. To do that, we must learn how to live in the conscious awareness that he is with us. God is your refuge and he is your strength. He is most definitely present in your life, when times are great, when times are tempting and every time in between.

A great way to end your time of prayer is to affirm that God is always with you and that you need his help. "Holy, heavenly Father, please show me today how I can overcome every temptation to sin against you that comes my way. Make me quick to realize the temptation and strong to turn from it so that I will honor you in every action and reaction. You are my escape when my old nature wants to sin, so remind me of your words and your truths and strengthen me in the core of my being to not get sucked into that same sin again. Protect me from myself, from the negative influences of others and from the enticements of the Evil One."

Some temptations are long and regular. That's why the passage says that God will provide us a way of escape so that we can endure the temptation. You can prevail and persevere through continuous waves of temptations. You can stand strong against the same temptation that's been dogging you for years. But you can't do it on your own. You need God to be your very present help in those times of temptation. You need to acknowledge that he is with you and he is for you and that you can overcome it through Christ who strengthens you.

Maybe the best discipline that you can learn is to live in the constant awareness of God's presence. Develop the habit of thinking about God throughout the day. Take control of your thinking to remind yourself that you live every moment under his watchful eye. Realize that you don't ever do anything with another person one on one. A third person is ever present, the Spirit of Jesus. That's why Jesus referred to him as our *Helper* (John 14:26). The Greek word can also be translated intercessor, advocate, consoler or comforter. It literally means "called to one's side".

Jesus' outline for us is how he wants us to pray. This

doesn't mean that you can't pray other ways or that you can't begin in the middle of this prayer outline as the need arises. If you have just sinned then jump right into confessing the sin and then checking your heart to determine if you have forgiven everyone who owes you something. Realize that this outline is the powerful weapon that Jesus gave us to use regularly, when we carve strategic time out of our schedules to talk with our heavenly Father.

Commit this outline to memory. Write it in your own words if that helps you. Keep it taped on your sun visor or to your mirror or laptop screen. Do whatever you need to do to commit this outline of prayer to memory so that you can enjoy the fullness of the abundant life that Jesus came to give us.

For the rest of this book, we'll study five Kingdom Come Prayers or KCP's for short. This is without a doubt the most misunderstood, the most under-applied and the most powerful part of Jesus' outline for our praying. It's very natural for us to go to God in prayer when life is hard. We're quick to pray to him when finances are lacking, sickness comes or relationships are crumbling. The Kingdom Come prayers are very different because they prepare us to face life's challenges from God's perspective. The Kingdom Come prayers are about lives being aligned with Jesus' way of thinking. Your challenge is to understand and own each of these prayers so that you can, very naturally and consistently, ask God for what he wants to give you, his Spirit.

Before moving on, work on owning and memorizing Jesus' prayer outline. You will find it on page 55. I recommend that you cut this page out and keep it with you to help you commit this outline to memory.

Small Group Questions

1. How were you taught to use what is called "The Lord's Prayer"? How has your understanding of it changed?

2. Look at the outline on page 55 again and discuss why you think Jesus chose this specific order of requests.

3. Read Matthew 6:14-15, how Jesus concluded his teaching on the prayer outline in the early months of his public ministry. How does this statement align with Matthew 18:23-35?

4. Why do you find it difficult to forgive people of what they owe you? By focusing on Jesus' story and the debt ratio, what can you do going forward to forgive as you have been forgiven?

5. Read 1 Corinthians 10:6-13. How do we put Christ to the test? Why is v12 in this passage? What are some practical ways that you can escape temptations?

The Followers' Prayer Outline – Luke 11:2-4

1st Thank your holy, heavenly Father

2nd Ask for his kingdom to come

3rd Ask for needs to be met

4th Confess specific sins and forgive everyone

5th Acknowledge his presence & power to protect

Chapter 3 - Kingdom Come Prayer #1 Spiritual Light

I do not cease to give thanks for you, remembering you in my prayers, that the God of our Lord Jesus Christ, the Father of glory, may give you the Spirit of wisdom and of revelation in the knowledge of him, having the eyes of your hearts enlightened, that you may know what is the hope to which he has called you, what are the riches of his glorious inheritance in the saints, and what is the immeasurable greatness of his power toward us who believe, according to the working of his great might that he worked in Christ when he raised him from the dead and seated him at his right hand in the heavenly places, far above all rule and authority and power and dominion, and above every name that is named, not only in this age but also in the one to come. And he put all things under his feet and gave him as head over all things to the church, which is his body, the fullness of him who fills all in all.

This first Kingdom Come Prayer comes from the above passage, Ephesians 1:16-23. Take a moment to read it again. It's one of the most majestic prayers in the

Bible. That's because it comes out of one of the most amazing passages in the Bible, Paul's opening verses of his letter to the believers of the church in the ancient city of Ephesus. If you have a Bible handy, read through vs1-23 of Ephesians before you continue this chapter.

Whenever you read one of the letters to the churches, you'll want to do so as if you are reading it with all of the members of your own church. These letters, called the Epistles, were first and foremost written to churches, to all the believers in those cities, as they gathered together to worship and learn. We tend to read these portions of Scripture as a personal letters to ourselves from God, and they are indeed that, secondly. They are however, first and foremost, letters to the gathered believers and thus we need to understand them in that context, as if we are all reading it together and considering the implications for the group. This proper understanding of the letters makes a huge difference in how we understand and apply the truths therein.

It is helpful to remember, too, that each word written comes from the inspiration of the Holy Spirit. This portion of Ephesians is exceptionally majestic and grandiose in describing how God has poured out his grace on us. It is surprising that the Spirit refers to Jesus as God's mystery. The specific words that the Spirit inspired Paul to write were intentional. It is important that we understand them. It is also freeing to admit that, at times, the words can also be very intimidating and difficult to understand. The prayer itself has a majesty and richness all its own. That is why we must explore it fully in order to be able to own it personally.

Over the years, theologians and scholars have grown in their understanding of the original Greek language. So much more is known about the language now than even

100 years ago. Thousands of manuscripts have been discovered in recent years. We have no copies of the original texts of either the Old or New Testaments. All of the manuscripts that we do have help us to confirm the exact content of the original writings. The many English translations we have today typically come from the same Greek translation, which is a compilation of the manuscripts, however the English translators use different words and phrases to try to capture the original meaning of the Greek and Aramaic. Because our English language is constantly changing and evolving, new Bible translations are continually being produced. Some translations focus more on finding the closest "word for word" meaning, while others emphasize a "thought for thought" philosophy. I have chosen the English Standard Version (ESV) for most passages due to its "essentially literal" translation style.

Depending on the translation you use, it is sometimes difficult to tell if this prayer in Ephesians has one request or multiple requests. The most reputable scholars today agree that the prayer you just read is actually one request to God with three incredible results.

THE REQUEST - He gives his Spirit

The request is this, *that the God of our Lord Jesus Christ, the Father of glory, may give you the Spirit of wisdom and of revelation in the knowledge of him.* Paul was led by the Spirit to continually intercede for the believers in each of the new churches. Some of these churches were started by Paul and others he came to after their inception to teach and strengthen their faith. Paul always traveled with other teachers, ministering together as a team. What is clear is that he and his team continually and faithfully prayed for the churches. They knew that the these churches desperately needed God's help through his Spirit to be able to survive. His primary request was that the Father would give them his Spirit so that they could know God better and better. God wanted those believers to continually increase in their understanding of his Word and his ways, just as he wants for you and me. God's desire for us is to know him better and better so that we will trust him more faithfully and love him in deeper devotion.

If you think about it, it makes perfect sense. Of course our Creator and Savior wants us to know him better. He wants us to understand him, as much as is humanly possible. He wants us to know that he is completely trustworthy and that he is always working for what is best for us and his kingdom. He wants us to believe that every word he has given us in the Bible comes from him, and it is all true. Your heavenly Father longs for you to *want* to know him so well that you can't stop asking him to help you do just that. He wants you to be able to understand the Bible as you read it so that you can apply it throughout every day. God wants to fill our hearts and minds with his Spirit's wisdom and insights so that we can grow in our knowledge and understanding of him.

The idea of knowing God intimately can be intimidating. How can a simple human like you possibly know Yahweh deeply and intimately? How can the One who created stars and galaxies, who sustains atoms and celestial orbits, be intimately known, like a loving father?

Is there someone who intimidates you? Often those who hold high positions in companies, government or in the entertainment and sports industries seem almost unknowable. They are super intimidating because they are so well known or so influential. I remember the day so vividly when I shared the elevator with the CEO. It was just the two of us and I was caught totally off guard. I remembered he loved professional baseball and was involved in raising money to rebuild the local stadium. To gain points, I made some comment about the team that was ridiculously obvious. I felt like an idiot. "Beam me up Scotty!" My face turned bright red and my palms erupted in a river of nervous sweat. Thankfully, my floor was well below the executives' suite so my terribly awkward ride was brief. Don't you hate it when that happens? People who hold power or prestige often intimidate the rest of us.

How about with you and God? Does speaking with him intimidate you so much that you rarely do it because you just don't know what to say to the Creator and Sustainer of the universe? If you knew him better, you would have more confidence to talk with him more naturally and more regularly. Praying would be a privilege. It would be much more natural and enjoyable to pray. So what's the answer? You and I need to get to know God better.

The great news is that this is his will for you. More than anything, God wants you to know him really well. He wants you to be more comfortable and more confident in his presence. He doesn't want you to pretend you know him and call him silly names like the Big Man Upstairs. We are to hold God in the utmost reverence and respect. At the same time, he wants us to open our hearts to him and pour out our cares on him, just like we would a trusted friend. *You are my friends if you do what I command you. No longer do I call you servants, for the servant does not know what his master is doing; but I have called you friends, for all that I have heard from my Father I have made known to you.* (John 15:14-15)

By believing that Jesus is the Lord of your life, you are his friend. As his friend, he wants to teach you all about his most gracious and glorious Father. He loves his Father with an unwavering devotion and he loves you as a brother/sister and a dear friend. Of course he wants you to know all about his Father. Jesus knows that as you get to know his Father better, you will grow in your loving devotion to him. That is Jesus' ultimate purpose, that you love his Father as much as he does.

In the Kingdom Come Prayer in Ephesians 1:17, the word that the Spirit led Paul to use is a special word for knowledge. It's a compound word that adds a prefix to the normal word for knowledge. Therefore, it's not just knowledge, but full, complete and precise understanding. The prefix helps to convey that God wants us to have a very personal and intimate understanding of who he is and what he is like. You have many acquaintances that you know, but you probably only have a few close friends that you know really well. What if you knew God as well as you know your closest friend?

Jesus used this compound word when he described how much he and the Father know each other. "*All things have been handed over to me by my Father, and no one knows the Son except the Father, and no one knows the Father except the Son and anyone to whom the Son chooses to reveal him.*" (Matthew 11:27) The Father and the Son have this complete and intimate knowledge of each other. They know each other so well that they are always one, in total unity in their actions and desires. Jesus explained his closeness with the Father by saying things like: "*I speak of what I have seen with my Father…*"(John 8:38) The Father wants us to get to know him in a similar way as his Son knows him.

How do we get to know God?

The request in this Kingdom Come Prayer is to ask the Father to help us know him better: *...that the God of our Lord Jesus Christ, the Father of glory, may give you the Spirit of wisdom and of revelation in the knowledge of him.* But how does that actually happen? You just read on the previous page that Jesus stated only those to whom he chooses to reveal the Father will ever know him. That is an amazing truth, but it can be confusing too.

Did you know that the only reason you believe in Jesus and can understand the Bible is that Jesus himself chose to reveal it to you? In the opening paragraphs, Paul reminded the believers in the church in Ephesus that God chose them before he even created the world. He adopted them into his family, forgave all their sins, purchased them out of slavery to self and Satan, and lavished his grace on them. Of course the exact same is true for you and me. Jesus made known to us the mystery of his Father's will – that all who believe in the Son for the forgiveness of their sins are rescued from the curse of death and hell. I recommend you pause now and read Ephesians 1:3-14 and 2:1-10 so that you can soak in the spiritual blessings that are yours in Christ.

The takeaway is that the only good in us comes from God and he continually saturates us in his grace. God's grace rescued you from sin and changed your mindset so that you could believe in Jesus. It is God's grace that enables you to do what is right and reject what is wrong. He is the one working in and through you to bring his Light into the lives of those you interact with each day.

Jesus said that he reveals his Father to people. He makes known to us who his Father is and what is really true in this life and the one to come. Jesus gives us enlightenment and understanding. The Greek verb translated "reveal" is *apokalypto.* As a noun, it's typically translated "revelation". "Apocalypse" is a direct transliteration from this Greek word. To Jesus' audience, when they heard the word apocalypse, they pictured something coming to light that was previously hidden or not understood. The last book of the Bible is The Revelation of Jesus Christ. Apocalypse isn't about aliens invading earth or giant meteors barreling toward us, it's the unveiling of God's truth to his people. God even tells us that the only way people can understand the Bible is if he gives them the ability to understand it. Otherwise, people's minds are veiled to its truths. On their own, without his help, they can't comprehend it's meaning. (2 Corinthians 4:1-6) We'll come back to this verse later in the chapter.

It is through the Spirit

Back to the prayer request. We are to ask the Father to give us his Spirit, who has all wisdom and revelation. That is how we came to know and believe in Jesus initially and that is the only way we can continue to grow closer to him. The Spirit of God gives us understanding as he opens our minds and hearts to the truths that we read in the Bible. That is what God wants you to ask him to do! His will for you is to give you all the wisdom and insight you need to be able to follow him with an undivided heart. He wants you to want what he wants for you, to know him better.

The only way to understand God is through the Spirit's help. Do we need more of the Spirit? Yes and no. When you received Jesus as your Lord and Savior, you were regenerated, or born from above. The phrase can also be translated "born again", but it seems to make more sense in light of the prophecies of the New

Covenant to think of it as "born from above". The Spirit of God renewed your heart and regenerated your spirit so that you became a new creation in Christ. Your identity is now in Christ Jesus. You belong to him because you were adopted into his family. The Father gave you to his Son as a cherished gift. These statements are all synonymous ways that the Bible describes the miracle of a person being forgiven of all their sins. Jesus described the new birth that must happen in John 3:1-21.

When you were *born of God* (1 John 3:9) you were made righteous by Christ and you were given the Holy Spirit to live within you. That's why Jesus told his disciples that it was better if he left, because only then could the Spirit come to live within them. Therefore we know that it is better to have the Spirit living within us than it is to have lived with Jesus back in the first century. We must get our minds around this fact that Jesus is always with us because his very Spirit lives in us.

This is the difference between the two covenants God gave. The First Covenant to the Jews was dependent on them faithfully keeping God's laws. Knowing they never would, because of man's sinfulness, he promised a New Covenant. The new one would be radically different from the first one. Here's what the Spirit revealed to the prophet Ezekiel hundreds of years before Jesus came to earth; *And I will give you a new heart, and a new spirit I will put within you. And I will remove the heart of stone from your flesh and give you a heart of flesh. And I will put my Spirit within you, and cause you to walk in my statutes and be careful to obey my rules.* (Ezekiel 36:26-27)

Ezekiel and other prophets (Jeremiah 31:31-40) predicted that God would do a miraculous work of giving his people a new heart and putting his Spirit within them so they would be able to obey him. But a perfect blood sacrifice had to be given to ratify the New Covenant. This is why Jesus said that the New Covenant is in his blood. Every time you participate in The Lord's Supper, you are remembering how God fulfilled his promise of long ago by sacrificing his Son, the Lamb of God, and giving us his Spirit to live within us for the rest of our lives.

Doesn't the prayer request make even more sense now? God made you his own so that you could know him intimately and have a vibrant and dependent relationship with your heavenly Father. Instead of as in human relationships where the older we get the more we grow independent from our parents, in Christ we grow more and more dependent on our Father the longer we live.

So does the Spirit come and go? Is that why we are to ask the Father to give us his Spirit? No. The Spirit doesn't leak out of us, but our faith sure leaks. Our commitment to Christ and our love for the Father definitely leaks. Therefore we need to be constantly renewed. The Spirit led Paul to write in Romans 12:2: *Do not be conformed to this world, but be transformed by the renewal of your mind, that by testing you may discern what is the will of God, what is good and acceptable and perfect.* The first Kingdom Come Prayer request is how we are transformed by the renewing of our minds. And we all need a ton of mind renewal! God knows this better than we do, so he gives us his Spirit in order to renew and transform how we think about life and God. He is in the business of giving his people the perspective of his Son. We can only get and maintain a right perspective through the Spirit's ongoing assistance as he shines his truth into our hearts and minds.

It's all about light

What existed before God created light? The Bible opens with; *In the beginning, God created the heavens and the earth. The earth was without form and void, and darkness was over the face of the deep. And the Spirit of God was hovering over the face of the waters.*

And God said, "Let there be light," and there was light. (Genesis 1:1-3)

Light seems to be one of God's favorite metaphors. Why? Because he created it. He is the one who imagined light and chose to make it become a reality. What a perfect metaphor it is! It is tangible and relatable so that every language group and all peoples throughout history have known the difference between dark and light. Dark hides what is true and real.

So how does God give us his Spirit of wisdom and revelation so that we can know him better? He shines the light of his truth into the dark places of our hearts and minds to make us see him. Without light you can't see. Without the Spirit bringing light to God's Word and our lives, we can't see to know God's will and what we should do or not do.

Let's return to the 2 Corinthians 4 passage: *And even if our gospel is veiled, it is veiled to those who are perishing. In their case the god of this world has blinded the minds of the unbelievers, to keep them from seeing the light of the gospel of the glory of Christ, who is the image of God. For what we proclaim is not ourselves, but Jesus Christ as Lord, with ourselves as your servants for Jesus' sake. For God, who said, "Let light shine out of darkness," has shone in our hearts to give the light of the knowledge of the glory of God in the face of Jesus Christ.* vs3-6

Think about this truth for a minute. God chose to shine in you the light of the knowledge of his glory, which is his Son, Jesus Christ. That means that he unveiled your dark mind to be able to understand and accept the truth of who Jesus is and what he offers to all who will receive him. I don't want to take the word for "knowledge" differentiation too far, but it's very interesting that the Spirit led Paul to use the regular word for knowledge here rather than the word for full and intimate knowledge. God shines into our hearts the general knowledge and understanding of who Jesus is. From this point on in our lives, he wants to give us more intimate knowledge of himself, his Son and his Spirit. The theological term for this growth and mind renewal transformation is sanctification.

Your heart's eyes

This Kingdom Come Prayer request in Ephesians 1:18 identifies exactly how the Father will help us to know him more fully: *having the eyes of your hearts enlightened, that you may know…* The heart is where all of our emotions and our desires live. This phrase of clarification was included in the prayer request so that we would know what needs to happen in our most inward part.

Isn't it interesting how the Spirit led Paul to word this phrase? What are the eyes of our hearts? It is a vivid metaphor of how our emotions and our deep-seated desires are wrongly influenced, darkened by our sinful nature. The only way to see what is right and what is wrong is if God sheds his light into our darkness. The eyes of the human heart are blinded and can only be given sight by God's gracious miracle. The Lord is illustrating how our innermost being needs to be fully enlightened to the words and ways of God. So we are to ask our Father to give us his Spirit, who has all wisdom and revelation, who can give clarifying light to our heart's eyes. We can also think of it as God's Spirit correcting our lenses with a new prescription that gives us sharp, 20/20 vision.

But it's not like you have 62% of the Spirit in you and you need to increase to 83%. You have 100% of the Spirit living within you. But does he have 100% of you? No, of course not! None of us are there. As long as we live on this sin-saturated earth, we'll never give ourselves fully to the Spirit, 24/7. Progress is definitely God's will for us. He wants us to desire to give ourselves fully to his Spirit. We're all on the same journey of growing into the kind of people who are increasingly influenced by the Spirit of God. What you and I need more than anything else is to be more influenced by the Spirit of God throughout every moment of every day.

The Epistles, the fancy name for the letters to the churches in the New Testament, are almost exclusively about teaching Jesus' followers how to follow him with absolute devotion. They interpret and apply Jesus' teachings for us with illustrations like: *And do not get drunk with wine, for that is debauchery, but be filled with the Spirit, addressing one another in psalms and hymns and spiritual s, singing and making melody to the Lord with your heart, giving thanks always and for everything to God the Father in the name of our Lord Jesus Christ, submitting to one another out of reverence for Christ.* (Ephesians 5:18-21)

Most of us know what it's like to be drunk. I'll spare you from going into a lot of personal testimony about my knowledge of intoxication. When you're drunk, you are not in control of yourself. You say and do things that you would never say and do otherwise. It's a very appropriate analogy. Instead of being under the influence of alcohol, or weed or drugs, God tells us to live under the growing influence of the Spirit of Jesus. As you ask the Father to give you more and more of his Spirit's influence in you, you'll do more of the kinds of things described in the passage above. You will live in thankfulness to God for everything good in your life, even joyfully submitting to others, putting them ahead of yourself, because you are in awe of Jesus. When you really put others ahead of yourself, that is when you know you are under the influence of the Spirit. Being under his control is also described in the Bible as being filled with the Spirit or being led by the Spirit. They are the same. Your goal in life is to live each day with the Spirit's help. *But I say, walk by the Spirit, and you will not gratify the desires of the flesh…If we live by the Spirit, let us also keep in step with the Spirit.* (Galatians 5:16 & 25) I like to picture in my mind that I'm following the Spirit so closely that if he suddenly stops, I'll bump right into him.

The more you are given the Spirit by the Father and influenced by him, you will experience the byproduct of the Spirit that is described in the verses that are in between the verses we just read from Galatians 5: *But the fruit of the Spirit is love, joy, peace, patience, kindness, goodness, faithfulness, gentleness, self-control; against such things there is no law. And those who belong to Christ Jesus have crucified the flesh with its passions and desires.* (Galatians 5:22-24)

The Spirit persuades you to love others more than you love yourself. When you really do put others interests ahead of your own, it's because you are being led by the Spirit of Christ. When you are genuinely patient and kind to others, it's because of the Spirit's influence in you. People are patient and kind every day without the help of the Spirit of God, but their motive isn't from God. They are likely doing it for what they might get out of that action, how it will benefit them or their reputation. But when you're drunk on the Spirit, he will lead you to be faithful to God. He will empower you to have self-control in the face of that temptation that often takes you down.

Here is how you can word this prayer request to make it a bit easier to own: "I ask you, the glorious Father of my Lord Jesus Christ, to give me your Spirit, who has all wisdom and revelation, to help me know you more fully by enlightening my heart's eyes to know..."

Three results

The rest of the passage reveals what God wants to accomplish through this one prayer request. There are three results, each of which can radically change your life: *that you may know* (1) *what is the hope to which he has called you,* (2) *what are the riches of his glorious inheritance in the saints, and* (3) *what is the immeasurable greatness of his power toward us who believe.* All of these are possible when the Father gives his people his Spirit to know him better, shining the light of his truth into their hearts.

Let's consider the three results one by one. Remember, this type of praying is what Jesus meant when he taught us to pray "*Your kingdom come.*" These Kingdom Come Prayers are all cause and effect requests. God teaches us to ask him for something specific so that he can bring about certain changes in our lives in order for us to be better aligned with his kingdom ways.

Kingdom Come Praying is an entirely different way of asking the Father for his help. This kind of praying involves the Spirit working within our hearts and minds to change us. As we think about what changes in our lives are needed, we can then ask for his help accordingly. Therefore we can approach these prayers from two different angles. We can recognize what is lacking in our lives, and pray the kind of request that will bring about that needed result. Or we can realize the request is what we desire, like in this prayer of knowing God better, and then enjoy the results that come from such a request. All of this will be much clearer as we work through this and the other Kingdom Come Prayers.

On that Thursday night before Jesus took on our sins and the punishment for those sins, he said this; "*If you abide in me, and my words abide in you, ask whatever you wish, and it will be done for you. By this my Father is glorified, that you bear much fruit and so prove to be my disciples.*" (John 15:7-8) Learning to pray according to the Bible is exactly how you keep Jesus' words abiding in you. Asking his Father to give us his Spirit so that we can know him better is a request that the Father wants to answer. It is his will for us. The Father will be glorified when you ask for him to give you his Spirit so that you can bear more and more fruit. The three results of this one request represent God-glorifying fruit that his followers will produce.

Let's look again at the request and the three results: *that the God of our Lord Jesus Christ, the Father of glory, may give you the Spirit of wisdom and of revelation in the knowledge of him, having the eyes of your hearts enlightened, that you may know what is the hope to which he has called you, what are the riches of his glorious inheritance in the saints, and what is the immeasurable greatness of his power toward us who believe,*

We are asking God to give us his Spirit so that we can know him more intimately and personally, so that we can understand and comprehend three critical truths. These are the three things that God wants us to understand about his kingdom as we get to know him better:

1. What is the hope of his calling
2. What are the riches of his glorious inheritance
3. What is the immeasurable greatness of his power

Read through these three results again. Notice who they belong to. It is God's hope and his inheritance and his power. We bring nothing to the table. The only thing we can give back to God is our loyalty and devotion. And that's all he requires.

Result #1 – You will know the hope of his calling

The Father wants you to understand: *what is the hope to which he has called you*. God the Father has called you into his hope. As the preceding verses in Ephesians 1 declare, God chose to adopt you and to make you understand that his will was to forgive your sins by punishing his Son in your place. That is the mystery of his will. And he chose to do that with people from every ethnicity and every language group.

This is our sure and certain hope. We have been rescued from standing before a holy God in self-defense. No one can stand before a holy God in self defense and win. The verdict will always be guilty and will always result in eternal separation from him. The crimes against God are all the sins people commit, the greatest being the rejection of his grace. The joy of our salvation is that we are judged righteous because of Jesus' righteousness. Because he has shown the light of his Truth, the Lord Jesus, into our hearts and we have believed him, we have an absolutely certain hope about our future.

The wonderful news about the certainty of our hope is that it has absolutely nothing to do with us. You can't earn it and you don't deserve it. The reason is simple. You didn't call yourself to God. You didn't just decide one day to be adopted into his family. God called you. He chose you. Our hope is his calling, not ours. That is why our hope is a rock-solid certainty. That is why we can know without an ounce of doubt that we live in his invisible presence on this earth and when we leave here, we will live in his visible presence forever.

Hope may be the greatest need of most people today. Hopelessness abounds in our world. It's shocking to think about the issues that teens deal with today compared to my teenage years in the 70's. Today's young people have to deal with pervasiveness of same sex temptations; cutting is prevalent; suicides are frequent; terrorism is unpredictable; and unprecedented domestic violence abounds. What does the trend of young people getting their bodies covered in tattoos tell us about their hope for the future? Surely body tattooing and piercing have something to do with a lack of hope. Is it not the uncertainty of life that leads young people to consider today only, and not think how they'll look in 30 years? Maybe many of them don't think they'll live that long. I'm not implying believers can't have ink. I am only questioning if the popularity of permanent body marking conveys some lack of hope for the future.

But followers of Jesus do have hope. And we have a way out when our hope fades. The solution is to cry out to your Father to give you his Spirit so that you can know him, having your heart flooded with the light of his promises so that you can comprehend the hope of his calling on your life.

When the Bible talks about hope, it isn't an uncertain wish, like "we hope it will all happen as God says". Our hope is certain and without question. Our hope is God's future, one that only he knows, but a future he has chosen to reveal to us.

When he tells us that he wants us to know the hope of his calling, he wants us to not be afraid of the future, or the present. Our loving Father wants us to trust him and believe that he is in absolute control – especially when circumstances steal our hope and joy. We not only have this sure hope that God is with us and that he is for us, we also know for certain that our eternal future is secure.

When the New Testament mentions hope, it especially emphasizes our eternal hope of being free from God's judgment for our sins. Galatians 5:5 reads: *For through the Spirit, by faith, we ourselves eagerly wait for the hope of righteousness.* This verse is referring to the righteousness that will be ours when Jesus returns, sin is eradicated and the new earth is created. Our struggle against sin will be forever removed and we will live in the fullness of God's righteous rule and reign in a life that will bring only love, joy and fulfillment. For believers who are currently suffering excruciating trials, they know the sure hope of the life that awaits them. That is what they are hanging to. The Epistles speak about this hope frequently because those first believers were under constant persecution for their faith in Jesus. For those of us whose lives are less threatening, it's more difficult to have an eternal focus on the life to come because life here is pretty darn good. We have to work harder at having a truly eternal focus. Kingdom Come Praying will help you to think more about God and his eternity.

In Ephesians 4:1 & 4 Paul wrote: *I therefore, a prisoner for the Lord, urge you to walk in a manner worthy of the calling to which you have been called…There is one body and one Spirit – just as you were called to the one hope that belongs to your calling.* Remember, God tells us that he called us out of a dark, hopeless life and into the glorious light of his Son's kingdom. He called us out of a life separated from him and into a life in his family, where he is Lord and King. We are to live in such a way that our choices, actions and reactions are worthy of having been called into the Light. It's a good idea to think about how you are handling yourself at any given moment of the day and to ask yourself if you are acting like someone who has been lavished with God's grace and called to be his son or daughter. To think about how our moment by moment choices are worthy of God or not, we need the eyes of our hearts enlightened in our knowledge of God.

Our hope comes from God's calling. By calling us into his family and making us his very own sons and daughters, we now have a sure hope for the future, and the present. God wants you to ask him to give you his Spirit so that you will grow closer to him so that you will have confidence in the hope of him calling you to himself and all that his calling entails.

God has promised that he will wipe away all that is evil from this world, dry up every tear and eradicate all suffering and all injustice. He isn't going to just overhaul this broken world. He's promised to create a new world, a new paradise for us to live with him in his visible presence. That is our inheritance. What a hope that is!

Of course it's super difficult to imagine. My view about heaven for a long time was a bunch of winged angel-like people singing hymns non-stop. That didn't sound too much like heaven at all. As a matter of fact, that seemed more like hell to me. Sorry, but as a young adult, that's exactly how I felt about heaven. I had a terribly wrong picture of the new world to come. God wants us to be excited about our forever lives with him in an ageless age. It will be so amazing that we cannot begin to comprehend the reality of it. But imagine your very best day, the most excited you've ever been about a time in your life, and then biggie size that with a triple shot and a few 5 Hour Energy drinks. The most beautiful place you've ever visited and the most fulfilled moment you've ever experienced can't begin to compare with every moment you will experience living in the new earth with God. If the Grand Canyon, the Swiss Alps, the Caribbean and the Northern Lights are from a broken creation, imagine how the new earth will look! Sin will have no influence on nature.

Here's an interesting fact about God. When he first created the world and placed man in paradise, he gave him an assignment. *The LORD God took man and put him in the garden of Eden to work it and keep it.* (Genesis 2:15) Remember what we learned about "LORD". This is God's personal name. The first thing the personal God does with his first son, Adam, right out of the gate, is to put him to work! He made man to be a co-creator with him.

I can't imagine what kind of work was needed in the paradise of Eden, but it must have been the most fulfilling work a man has ever done. There were no Monday blues. Adam never dreaded going to work. And that's the kind of work we'll all be doing in the new earth, the most fulfilling and rewarding, creative work imaginable.

If you or someone you know is feeling hopeless, God has given us precisely what to request of him. All you have to do is learn how to ask God for what he wants to give. Simply ask the glorious Father of your Lord Jesus Christ to give you his Spirit of wisdom and revelation so that you can know God more personally and then better understand the hope of his calling on your life. He has to answer this request. He will do it. But you must ask and keep on asking and seek and keep on seeking and knock and keep on knocking. Your Father who loves you wants to give you his Holy Spirit.

Here are some of the truths that spring from the hope of his calling:

- The moment you die, you will be with him
- You are completely forgiven of all of your sins
- God loves you and is for you
- Jesus will never forget about you
- Jesus is interceding for you, now
- The Father never forgets your prayer requests
- You already have every spiritual blessing
- He will give you the wisdom you need
- He will give you the strength you need
- His plans for your life have purpose
- He created you just the way he intended
- Everything in your life is working towards his purposes
- He will see you safely home, to be with him
- The Father knows everything that is happening
- You can overcome every temptation in Christ

I'll close this section on hope with one of the Bible's most beautiful blessings: *May the God of hope, fill you with all joy and peace in believing, so that by the power of the Holy Spirit you may abound in hope.* (Romans 15:13)

Result #2 – You will know his inheritance

The second result that our Father wants us to fully comprehend is also in v18; *what are the riches of his glorious inheritance in the saints.* God wants you to know him more intimately so you can better comprehend the riches of his glorious inheritance. Hope and inheritance are inseparable. Our hope is that the promised inheritance will come about. Our certainty that it will happen exactly as God has said in the Bible and that some celestial lawyer won't be able to overturn our receiving this inheritance comes from the fact that it is God's inheritance.

The wording is a bit surprising. You would think that it is our inheritance that we receive in the new world. That's how we think about inheriting money or possessions here on earth. Your wealthy family member dies and leaves you money, land, property, etc. It is your inheritance. But God surprises us. He says that it is actually his inheritance *in the saints.* It's not just his inheritance, it is *the riches of his glorious inheritance* that he wants us to know all about and have confidence that it will most definitely be ours. Remember, we are God's own possession. He bought us with the price of his Son's life. When the end comes, God will have all of his purchased people with him. Jesus will live forever with every soul that the Father has given to him. The Spirit will have every person who has been born from him. (John 3:5-8) We are also God's inheritance! He will inherit the work of his grace over the span of history to have every man, woman and child he has delivered living with him in his glorious kingdom. He will show us just how truly majestic, loving and full of splendor he is.

In Genesis 12, we read about God calling a man out of his home town and leading him to a new place. God gave him a promise of inheriting a vast land and that from his lineage, a great nation would emerge. It was the land where God's people were to live under his reign so that they could show all of the other nations how to live as God's people. The man was Abram, whose name was later changed to Abraham, and the nation was the Jews. The land was Israel. This promise of a new land where his people would live is the core of the First Covenant. Their inheritance wasn't just the land itself, but it included all of the cities and homes and farms and riches that were already in the land. The Jews' inheritance was massive.

Our inheritance is pictured in the Promised Land of the Jews. God is going to recreate the world and the imagery in the Revelation is one of a massive city, the new Jerusalem, coming down from heaven to be the capital of the world. In this revelation that Jesus gave to the old apostle John, he described the brilliance of the city and said that the new earth will have no need of a sun or moon like our world. The glory that radiates from the Father and the Son will be the city's light.

Read the description of God's promised inheritance from Revelation 21:1-7 several times and take time to soak it in and to ponder the reality of it.

> *Then I saw a new heaven and a new earth, for the first heaven and the first earth had passed away, and the sea no longer existed. I also saw the Holy City, new Jerusalem, coming down out of heaven from God, prepared like a bride adorned for her husband.*
>
> *Then I heard a loud voice from the throne:*
> *Look! God's dwelling is with humanity,*
> *and He will live with them.*
> *They will be His people,*
> *and God Himself will be with them*
> *and be their God.*
> *He will wipe away every tear from their eyes.*
> *Death will no longer exist;*
> *grief, crying, and pain will exist no longer,*
> *because the previous things have passed away.*
>
> *Then the One seated on the throne said, "Look! I am making everything new." He also said, "Write, because these words are faithful and true." And He said to me, "It is done! I am the Alpha and the Omega, the Beginning and the End. I will give water as a gift to the*

thirsty from the spring of life. The victor will inherit these things, and I will be his God, and he will be My son."

All of the challenges and hassles and hardships of life on planet earth will be remembered no more. There will be no crime, no wars, no disease, no suicide, no cutting, no immorality, no hatred, no wars, no jealousy, no back-stabbing, no loneliness, no gender confusion, no feelings of inferiority, no prejudices, no depression – only love, joy, peace, patience, kindness, goodness, faithfulness, gentleness and self-control. On the cross, Jesus defeated enemy number one, sin.

Our Guarantee

"But how do I know for sure this will all happen and that I'll be included?" I'm so glad you asked. We have a guarantee. We have an eternal membership card that can never be lost or made void. We have been forever sealed with this guarantee and the guarantee is a person. He is the Holy Spirit. He is our certainty.

> *God's purpose was that we Jews who were the first to trust in Christ would bring praise and glory to God. And now you Gentiles have also heard the truth, the Good News that God saves you. And when you believed in Christ, he identified you as his own by giving you the Holy Spirit, whom he promised long ago. The Spirit is God's guarantee that he will give us the inheritance he promised and that he has purchased us to be his own people. He did this so we would praise and glorify him.* (Ephesians 1:12-14, NLT)

Our hope of God's inheritance in the saints is based on his promise. Does God always keep his promises? Of course he does!

Let's run down a short rabbit trail. God wants us to

keep asking him to help us know him better so that we can understand all about his inheritance *in the saints*. Did you know that you are a saint? Saints are not those who live extraordinary lives as followers of Christ and after they die, get their own statue. Honoring wonderful role models is great and we should do that. But to dub someone a saint because they have done extraordinary things is completely wrong, according to the Bible. Every person that God has called to be his own is a saint. The word "saint" is the adjective of the noun "holy". Holy means "set apart" or "other". Every believer in Christ has been set apart by God to be his very possession. God is holy and since we are his and in Christ, we too are holy. The way you live does not make you a saint, or un-saint! We are only saints because we belong to Christ Jesus. It is our identity as the children of God. …*giving thanks to the Father, who has qualified you to share in the inheritance of the saints in light.* (Colossians 1:12) Hebrews 11:15 reiterates this truth again: *Therefore he* (Jesus) *is the mediator of a new covenant, so that those who are called may receive the promised eternal inheritance, since a death has occurred that redeems them from the transgressions committed under the first covenant.* The death is, of course, Jesus' death.

So the inheritance will be totally shared among all believers. Sharing inheritance doesn't usually work too well in families in our world. Why is that? It is due to the sins of jealousy, coveting and selfishness. Where none of these sins exist, sharing the inheritance will not only be possible, all of us equally sharing the glorious riches in the new world will be exactly what each of us will want to do! Now that's exceedingly cool to think about.

To solidify our thinking about God's hope and his inheritance, let's turn to the Spirit's inspiration to the apostle Peter. *Praise the God and Father of our Lord Jesus*

Christ. According to His great mercy, He has given us a new birth into a living hope through the resurrection of Jesus Christ from the dead and into an inheritance that is imperishable, uncorrupted, and unfading, kept in heaven for you. You are being protected by God's power through faith for a salvation ready to be revealed in the last time. (1 Peter 1:3-5, HCSB)

This is the inheritance that your Father wants you to know all about so that it can lift you up in times of discouragement. Knowing all about and believing with confidence in this coming inheritance can greatly impact your priorities and how you value the things of this life. How do you grow in your understanding of this inheritance? How can the reality of the forever life that's coming drain the dread of what you're dealing with now? Do what God says. Ask him to give you his Spirit of wisdom and revelation so that you can get to know God better as he sheds light on your emotions regarding this future inheritance that is kept in heaven for you. When you get overwhelmed with the cares of this world and all the things that require your energies, ask the Father to give you his Spirit so you can refocus on what really matters. After all, the only thing that will be in God's new world that is currently in our world is his people. Your house, car, job, phone, insurance and 401k will all be gone one day.

Result #3 – You will know his power

At this point in his praying, the apostle Paul seems to have been overcome with the splendor of the majesty that is ours in Christ. It's as if there weren't enough words or the right words, for him to properly describe the benefits for us in asking the Father to give us his Spirit. The 3rd result in its entirety is found in vs19-23, that we will know *what is the immeasurable greatness of his power toward us who believe, according to the working of his great might that he worked in Christ when he raised him from the dead and seated him at his right hand in the heavenly places, far above all rule and authority and power and dominion, and above every name that is named, not only in this age but also in the one to come. And he put all things under his feet and gave him as head over all things to the church, which is his body, the fullness of him who fills all in all.*

Wow! Read it again. Read it one more time. Good granny! What a truth this is. It's so big that the Spirit led Paul to use four different words for power. Circle "power" in the first line of this passage. From that Greek word we get the English word dynamite. Circle "working". The Greek word translated working is "energeian". It's God's energy that is doing the work. Next, circle the word "might". This word is also translated power, dominion and strength. Lastly, circle "worked". This word is yet another Greek word for ability, force, strength or might. A very literal translation of the phrase is: *what is the infinite mega power toward us…according to the energy of his great strength that he forced in Christ.* What message is God trying to convey to us?

Read the first phrase again. God doesn't want us to just know his power that it available to us, he wants us to know how immeasurably great his power is. He wants us to understand that his power is exceedingly, incomparably, incredibly and surpassingly great. The Greek word for great is mega. God wants you to know how infinitely mega powerful he is and that his power is ready to be used in your life.

As you and I get to know God more intimately and trust him more faithfully, we'll also understand more of the magnitude of his limitless power that is ready and waiting to be used on our behalf. He tells us that it is the very same power that God flexed when he raised Jesus from the dead and put him in the place of ultimate authority. This lofty passage helps us to better understand that it took God's unlimited energy to bring about the resurrection of Jesus. It wasn't that the Father could just snap his fingers and make Jesus alive again. God was conquering sin and death. He overcame Satan and all of his demons (yes, they are all real, just as you, me and Jesus are real). This passage helps us to understand the fullness and the magnitude of the power of God that was required to bring the Lamb of God back to life. We should be able to appreciate the resurrection of Jesus better as we ask God to give us his Spirit so that we can more fully comprehend his power.

His matchless power

You can be set free from fears about wars, terrorism and political scandals by focusing on the reality of God's power and Jesus' authority. Jesus controls all that happens in the seen world and the unseen world. You don't have to worry about demons or Satan or their influence over you. But if you find yourself worrying about evil and the Evil One, ask your loving heavenly Father to give you his Spirit of wisdom and revelation so you that can be assured of his absolute reign. Jesus rules and reigns over everything and everyone in the spirit realm and in our world too. We need God's help through his Spirit to keep those truths in the forefront of our cerebral matter.

Iran will only be able to create nuclear warheads if Jesus allows it. North Korea will only grow in power if Jesus permits them to. Russia is under Jesus' authority to only do what he lets them to do. That's just the way it is! We have so many examples in the Scriptures of God raising up leaders and bringing them down, all according to his will and his plans. Nothing can thwart God from carrying out his plans, on a global scale and in your life too. You and I need to know this truth and we need to believe it is real. We need God's help every day to comprehend his magnificent power that is ours in Christ.

His strength for hard times

Some have been misled to believe that because of Christ's authority and power, faithful believers will be delivered from persecution and poverty. That is a terrible lie from the pit of hell and it smells like smoke. Having the fullness of God's incredible power available to you does not mean you won't face hardships, sickness and financial challenges. It does not mean you will never be made fun of for your faith. Having his power doesn't mean you will not face danger or terminal illness. Let's face it, we all have to die one way or another.

Jesus' people have been facing persecution, martyrdom, enslavement and every other hardship in life since his church was birthed in Jerusalem almost 2,000 years ago. Remember, it was John's faithful brother James, one of the inner three (Peter, James & John), who was murdered for his faith in Christ (Acts 12:1-2). Before him, one of the first deacons, Stephen, was stoned to death (Acts 7:54-60). Can you imagine having a crowd throw rocks at you until you die? Was God not powerful enough to stop either of these murders? We all know that answer, but we can find ourselves really confused at times, especially when very bad things happen to really good people. What makes it even tougher is when a non-believing friend or co-worker asks you why God let such a senseless tragedy happen at all.

God is always restraining evil, the darkness of Satan

and his kingdom and the evil that is part of our selfish human nature. He doesn't want any of the evil to happen, but he has created a world of choice and it is our choices that open the way for all kinds of evil. There are two kingdoms in this world. There is the dark kingdom of Satan and the light kingdom of Jesus (definitely not "lite" kingdom). Everyone is in either one camp or the other.

Those of us who have been called out of the dark domain and into the kingdom of light and life are so blessed and privileged. We are protected by God's power to be his people in a dark and dying world. We have his power working within us so that we can say no to every temptation and yes to living in Jesus' rightness. We have God's power so that we can overcome everything this world and the Evil One throws at us. We even have the power to be able to give up our life in order to stand in steadfast devotion to Jesus. Believers in persecuted countries do it every day. Followers of Christ are being persecuted and murdered every day because they belong to him. We must accept the reality of how evil our world actually is.

God's power to help us is essential to us living the abundant life Jesus promised. By abundance, he certainly was not referring to possessions, safety and health. Jesus gives us the abundant life of knowing *his* Father as *our* Father and belonging to him as his most treasured possession. The abundant life is Kingdom life and that life is fueled through our Kingdom Come Praying.

Jeremy Camp's song, "Same Power", was inspired by this prayer. Here is the chorus:

> The same power
> that rose Jesus from the grave
> The same power

that commands the dead to wake
Lives in us, lives in us
The same power
that moves mountains when he speaks
The same power
that can calm a raging sea
Lives in us, lives in us
He lives in us, lives in us

Let's get very practical with how the availability of God's power works in our lives. Let's say a friend of yours has an addiction to pornography, or maybe they are dealing with strong feelings toward the same sex, or maybe they're thinking about committing adultery or even suicide. One of the best things you can do, if not the very best, is to intercede for them. Pray this Kingdom Come Prayer for them, and keep on praying and keep on interceding for them until they are overcoming the temptation consistently. You will ask your glorious Father to give them his wise and revealing Spirit to shine in this dark place in their heart so that they can experience his power to resist the temptation each time it comes. Pray that the Spirit will show them how God's power is available to them to not only resist the temptations but to suppress even the thought of such an act. What they need is the power of God working in their life so that his energy replaces their weakness to this sin. They need the Spirit to reveal to them how evil these desires are, bringing light into their dark thinking, so that they can know the power of Christ to overcome.

Jesus talked a lot about conquering the darkness that surrounds us in Revelation Chapters 2-3. To each of the seven churches, he gave a captivating promise to everyone who conquers temptations to sin. We can only conquer temptations with the help of the power of God working in our hearts and minds. We must understand our desperate need for God and his Spirit to help us live lives that please him.

We all need God's power. We need to know that his power is available to us every time we call out to him. We need to know that God is working in and through us with his power even when we can't see what he is doing. We need to know that he's working when we don't think he is. We need his power to be able to wait. We can know all that we need to know about God's power in our lives by asking him to give us his all-knowing Spirit.

Therefore, my beloved, as you have always obeyed, so now, not only as in my presence but much more in my absence, work out your own salvation with fear and trembling, for it is God who works in you, both to will and to work for his good pleasure. (Philippians 2:12-13) God is at work in and through you. Asking him to give you his wise and revealing Spirit will open your eyes to understand more of how he is working. If you need to know the certainty of his hope or the riches of his inheritance or the immeasurable greatness of his power that is yours, ask him. Ask the Father, who loves you more than you can imagine, to give you his Spirit so that you can know him more personally and more deeply. Ask him for his help so that you can keep working out what he is working in you.

Grace be with all who love our Lord Jesus Christ with love incorruptible. (Ephesians 6:24)

Small Group Questions

1. Talk about how the Spirit has given you wisdom or a revelation of understanding in the past. Did you ask for it? How did it help you know God?

2. Discuss the analogy of being drunk versus being filled with the Spirit from Ephesians 5:18-21. What is the evidence of being filled? How have you recently experienced the Spirit's influence?

3. What stands out to you about our hope of salvation from Romans 8:18-25? What truths in vs26-30 encourage you to remain hopeful?

4. Discuss the many ways that God's inheritance for us is different than an inheritance on earth.

5. Read aloud the 3rd result from Ephesians 1:19-23. How does this reality encourage you that Philippians 4:13 is true for you too?

Kingdom Come Prayer #1

Ephesians 1:17-19

THE REQUEST

I ask you, the glorious Father of my Lord Jesus Christ, to give me your Spirit who has all wisdom and revelation, to help me know you more fully, having my heart flooded with your light…

1st Result

so that I might know what is the hope of your calling…

2nd Result

so that I might know what are the riches of your glorious inheritance in the saints…

3rd Result

so that I might know what is the immeasurable greatness of your power toward us who believe.

Chapter 4 - Kingdom Come Prayer #2
Spiritual Power

For this reason I bow my knees before the Father, from whom every family in heaven and on earth is named, that according to the riches of his glory he may grant you to be strengthened with power through his Spirit in your inner being, so that Christ may dwell in your hearts through faith - that you, being rooted and grounded in love, may have strength to comprehend with all the saints what is the breadth and length and height and depth, and to know the love of Christ that surpasses knowledge, that you may be filled with all the fullness of God.

This second Kingdom Come Prayer comes from Ephesians 3:14-19. Think for a moment about how the Spirit of God led the apostle Paul in writing this letter. Coming out of the first prayer in Chapter 1, he explained the immeasurable riches of God's grace to his people in forgiving their sins and making them to be his holy nation, members of God's very household. There is a strategic emphasis on the unity of Christ's Church, which is made up of a plethora of uniquely diverse local churches and individuals. Thankfully, many local churches today are becoming more diverse ethnically and socio-economically which rightly reflects the strength of our diversity. Until he returns to earth, Jesus is building his one Church, which is made up of millions of local churches from every nation and of all shapes and sizes.

The truths that Paul articulated so majestically between the two prayers are precisely what propels him into the second prayer. The first prayer was a request for the Father to give us his Spirit, who has all wisdom and revelation, so that we can know him more personally and thus better understand his hope, his inheritance and his power that is ours in Christ. The verses between the two prayers are exceedingly rich doctrines such as:

- We were dead to God because of our sins
- He saved us when we were in rebellion to him
- He has made his mystery known to us
- We could never earn his forgiveness
- We are rescued by his grace through faith
- We have been created as God's masterpiece
- We have been made to do good deeds
- We are being built up with all other believers
- Separated people are made one in Christ
- The people of God are in Christ Jesus
- We have bold, confident, direct access to God

It will be helpful for you to study the verses that bridge these two prayers. Like the first prayer, this second prayer has been interpreted differently, depending on the translators. Some take this passage as having multiple requests. None of these interpretations are inherently wrong. The original wording is quite technical which makes it difficult to know for certain.

Because of the close connection between the various phrases in the passage, it is probably best to understand this prayer as one request with three purpose clauses, similar to the first Kingdom Come Prayer we explored in the previous chapter of this book. Further reasoning for understanding the prayer as one request is found in the fourth Kingdom Come Prayer in Colossians 1:9-12. Ephesians and Colossians are parallel letters written by the apostle Paul, at the same time, from prison. The prayer in Colossians is much shorter, and it contains two requests: to be filled with the knowledge of God's will and to be strengthened with all of his power. We'll explore this prayer in Chapter 6. The Colossians' prayer represents a shorter version of the two prayers in Ephesians, as they share the same basic requests. The Ephesian prayers can also be considered one prayer with two parts that parallel the prayer in Colossians 1.

The Launchpad

The Spirit inspired Paul with very descriptive words in this beautifully worded, second Kingdom Come Prayer. I will refer to this prayer as the second prayer when most likely it is the second portion of Paul's continual prayer for the believers in the church in Ephesus. In Paul's diligent praying for those believers, he certainly would have combined the first prayer with this one. We can think of 1:22-3:13, the verses in between the two prayers, as the lettuce, tomatoes, cheese and ham of this delicious prayer sandwich. The two prayers are like bookends that hold between them some of the riches truths in all of Scripture.

The introduction to the second portion of the prayer is in 3:14-15: *For this reason I bow my knees before the Father, from whom every family in heaven and on earth is named.* For what reason? Why did Paul and his team focus so much of their time and emotional energies on praying for the believers in the various churches? The reason is that God has done a marvelous thing in rescuing people out of the dark domain and bringing them together, into his Son's kingdom, as his people. He knows each one's name and he knows their family's names. God's calling is very individualistic - by name. Each person is called out, by name, to become part of this gigantic and hugely diverse family. He knows us all by name! That is the wider reason.

Prior to these verses, the apostle wrote another amazing truth: *in whom we have boldness and access and confidence through our faith in him.* The whom and the him are of course, Jesus Christ. What this doctrine declares is that every believer has direct access to God the Father with bold assurance and unwavering confidence. We can be sure that he hears us and acts according to what is best for us and his kingdom. The Father listens to our prayers and works accordingly because we are in his Son. We are in a forever union with him and our faith is in him. Because we belong to Jesus, we can run to the Father at any time and tell him what's wrong. He always listens to his children!

The apostle also wrote that he bowed down to pray. This doesn't mean that bowing is the only stance we should take when praying. In Paul's day, the normal stance for praying was standing up. The Spirit influenced Paul and his team to often kneel when they prayed as a practical way of demonstrating their humility before God and their passion for the people for whom they were praying. Their commitment to these believers and deep dependence on their Lord frequently drove them to their knees for prayer.

Let me suggest that you practice different positions when you pray. As I've mentioned previously, you can pray anywhere and at any time. You can pray in the car or in a crowd. In the mornings, I usually sit on our sofa with a cup of coffee to read and pray. But we can learn much from our Savior, and from Paul and his team, by observing that they often got alone to pray. Sometimes Jesus prayed looking up to his Father in the heavens. In his most desperate prayer, Jesus began praying on his knees, but when he was overcome with grief, fell face down to beg for his Father's help. (Luke 22:42 & Matthew 26:39) Here in Ephesians, we read that Paul and his team often got down on their knees and bowed in prayer. No one way is right or wrong. It is good to change it up and it is good to let your body respond to what your heart is feeling. In my most challenging or depressing times, I have found that kneeling when I pray helps me to express my desperate dependence on my Father in the heavens. Let your body position and your attitude in prayer reflect your love and reverence for God and your deep dependence on him.

Because we have bold access with confidence, Paul bowed and prayed to the Father: *from whom every family in heaven and on earth is named.* Prayers are very personal. We are praying to our Father whose people span the entire history of mankind. Heaven is filled with worshipping saints who have gone before us and to whom we all share a common lineage. We're all the children of God, one family from many different families and many different ethnicities, all of which are named by God himself. There is no place for prejudices in the family of God. No person is better than any other and no family is more important than any other family. Maybe you've heard it said, the ground is level at the foot of the cross.

That's what the apostle Paul reiterated here, after explaining it so clearly in 2:11-21.

THE REQUEST - To be strengthened

The second Kingdom Come Prayer request is this: *that according to the riches of his glory he may grant you to be strengthened with power through his Spirit in your inner being.* This is the request the Father wants us to ask for. God wants you to ask him to make you mighty with power through his Spirit in the depth of your being. It is something that God grants to us as we ask him. He wants you to be mightier by his power. You must learn to ask him. It's that simple.

Notice how Paul added the conditional clause to this strengthening by God. He was reminded by the Spirit to state the source of our strengthening. What is this source? How are we empowered? The source is the riches of his glory. This phrase encapsulates the fullness and completeness of all of his attributes. God's desire is to apply all of his rich attributes in power to us for our spiritual transformation and renewal. It takes the power of God working mightily in our lives to bring about the changes he so desires. He uses two words for power to emphasize how much strengthening we really need. Paul prayed for believers *to be strengthened with power through his Spirit.*

It is a gift

There's another very critical emphasis in this prayer request. Empowerment is a gift. Paul didn't just pray that believers would be strengthened with power through the Spirit, although it's fine to ask in that way. Paul was led by the Spirit to ask specifically for God to grant this to happen. The word used here is the normal Greek word "to give". The noun form is "gift". The Spirit is emphasizing to us that this strengthening is a gift from God. It is a gift that he wants to give us as we ask him for it. It is so important for us to understand this that the Spirit led Paul to use the word "gift" a dozen times in this short letter. The Spirit is a gift (1:17), God's grace is a gift (3:2, 7, 8; 4:7, 8, 29) and his strengthening is a gift (3:16). Why does the Bible emphasize that everything good that we have is a gracious gift from God?

Too many times we slip back into the performance mindset that if we live just right or serve in Children's Ministries or give enough money to the church, God will give us his blessings. You can never earn God's blessings or his favor. You will never deserve them either. Our glorious heavenly Father gives us his grace and his power out of his steadfast love for us, *according to the riches of his glory.* As you ask God to strengthen you, always remember that it is his gift to you. You don't deserve his empowerment and you can't limit his strengthening by your failings. We can migrate to either end of a faith-killing continuum: to think we deserve his grace or to think we're so weak in our faith that he'll never bless us. You are his child. Our Father wants his children to understand that all they will ever need comes from his hands. He wants to give us everything that will be good for us and good for his kingdom. Therefore, ask him. Ask him to make you strong in his power through his Spirit. Don't ever feel that God won't strengthen you because you are so undeserving. That's exactly right. You are undeserving. But God is faithful. His love for you is steadfast and independent of your success in obeying. "Dear Father, from the riches of your glory, please grant me to be strengthened with your power through your Spirit in the depths of my soul."

The first request in Ephesians 1:17 is for God to give us his Spirit so that we can know him better. The second request here in 3:16 is for God to give us his Spirit so that we can be strong with his very power in our inner being. How will your life be better if you are being constantly strengthened and made wise by the indwelling Spirit of Christ?

From the inside out

The inner being represents the center of a person, the place where intelligence, desires, dreams and emotions are birthed. This is where the Spirit does his renewing and transforming work. Your inner self is the new you, where Christ lives in you, the real you. Paul wrote that we have been taught as followers of Jesus: *to put off your old self, which belongs to your former manner of life and is corrupt through deceitful desires, and to be renewed in the spirit of your minds, and to put on the new self, created after the likeness of God in true righteousness and holiness.* (Ephesians 4:22-24) He gave us this truth in the form of a metaphor we do every day – changing our clothes. Picture putting off the old self just like you would quickly get out of sopping wet, cold clothes. You can't get them off fast enough. The old self is to be thrown off so that the spirit of your mind, the new you, can be continually renewed in your thinking. The new you is being renewed into what it was originally created to be, in the likeness of God. The changes that God wants to bring about in you and me will make us more like him which means we will be very different in our thinking, compared to people who don't know God.

The fulfillment of the New Covenant, promised by the prophets of old, became reality in Christ: *Therefore, if anyone is in Christ, he is a new creation. The old has passed away;*

behold, the new has come. (2 Corinthians 5:17) It is no longer we who are living but it is actually Christ who lives in and through us. He is our source of life and our strength to live: *I have been crucified with Christ. It is no longer I who live, but Christ who lives in me. And the life I now live in the flesh I live by faith in the Son of God, who loved me and gave himself for me.* (Galatians 2:20) We have our identity in Christ and he is our new life and our real life: *For you have died, and your life is hidden with Christ in God.* (Colossians 3:3) The old you is gone. All of these are astounding truths that are sometimes tough to grasp. That is why you and I need more of the power of God in our inner most being, so that we can believe all of these realities of God and live them out on a consistent basis.

The part of you that stood condemned by God, because of your rebellion in sins, has been removed from you. It was crucified with Christ when he was crucified. That is why your salvation is certain and it can't be taken away due to your disobedience. You were born anew by the Spirit's regeneration. The new you is being renewed day by day, through the power of God. Of course, Jesus' desire is that you and I would want the same things for us that he wants, to be renewed into his likeness – to have his attitudes, actions and devotion to the Father. In Ephesians 5:1, the Spirit inspired Paul to write: *Therefore be imitators of God as beloved children.*

The needed changes to our attitudes, actions and allegiance are deep within our souls. Our transformation process is an inside-out revolution that happens by God's gracious power working within us. He gives us strength to deny temptations. He empowers us to be able to understand how to apply his Word to our lives. He makes us mighty in faith to stand on our convictions when others deny him. He strengthens us to be able to follow him as he leads us to do his kingdom work. He empowers spouses to hang in there when the marriage seems hopeless. He strengthens his people to endure with patience all kinds of hardships and hang-ups. Our actions are only reflective of what is happening in our heart. That is why Paul was inspired to ask God to give his people power through the Spirit deep within their very core.

My wife, Tammy, and I had achieved the Great American Dream – our own business, a house, two cars, two kids and a dog. We were fairly mature in our faith and continuing to grow in our understanding of God's will for our lives. But the day I came home from work and Tammy told me she felt like God was calling us to be missionaries – I mean, the kind of missionary that goes to a foreign county to live – well, I just about dropped dead. I rationalized that she must have gotten overly emotional at her women's Bible study (which was led by a missionary) and that this totally insane idea would soon pass. "Make it go away God! Please, please, please change her mind.", was my plea.

We committed to praying diligently about this for the next month. At that time, I was not familiar with the Kingdom Come Prayers, but I did understand how to ask him for his will and to give us clarity and unity. What I didn't realize was that God was working powerfully within me to change my heart and to give me the strength to say "yes" to this terrifying assignment. His power within the depths of my soul was completely overwhelming. Within a month, I was convinced that God did indeed want us to sell the business, sell our home, give up the bright financial future and go to seminary to prepare to minister wherever in the world it was that he had planned for us to go. After completing seminary, we spent six years in Senegal, West Africa with the mission organization SIM, sharing the fantastic news of forgiveness in Jesus Christ to the Muslims of that country, in their native language. Talking about power. He strengthened us to learn an African language so that we could explain to them the wonderful reality of Jesus' sacrifice for our sins. That, my friend, is the power of God working in the depths of the heart of his child!

Being strengthened to answer yes to a missionary calling isn't the norm. God's normal activity is to empower us daily to do the regular work of the Kingdom, like forgiving someone, showing patience, loving the unlovable and sharing our possessions. The power of God is evidenced by the kinds of attitudes and actions it produces in the hearts of his people. When you experience the impact of the Spirit in your life, it is because the power of God made you mighty to display these qualities. Sometimes, God gives us this internal strengthening without us even asking for it. That is how his grace works. However, his will for us is that we *ask* to have his power working within so that we can please him. He wants us to live in the reality of realizing how much we need his strength deep in our souls, so that we will keep asking him to supply it.

It's not about religion

Jesus was intensely opposed to religion. The difference between religion and faith in Christ is this: Religion is about doing righteous things. Faith in Christ is about becoming a righteous person. Religion demands right actions. Jesus makes possible a right relationship that will produce changed attitudes and actions. Every religion teaches that a person is declared good, that they can enter heaven or enjoy the after-life, if they do the right actions that are prescribed by that specific religion. Of course, those actions vary all over the place according to each religion. When Jesus began teaching, he sharply condemned the Jews because they practiced religion. They had long lists of the right things to do and the wrong things not to do. Their lists were derived from the Law of Moses but they missed its purpose and added hundreds of new traditions to the Law. The Law's purpose was to show God's holiness and man's sinfulness – mankind's absolute inability to keep God's Law.

Faith in Jesus is just the opposite. We can only come to receive Christ by acknowledging our spiritual bankruptcy. Coming to Christ means we understand how sinful we are and that Jesus' perfection is the only solution to our rebellion. Our faith in Jesus begins in the heart and continues growing there until we leave this earth. To describe his reality Jesus said, "*Blessed are the poor in spirit, for theirs is the kingdom of heaven.*" (Matthew 5:3) Understanding spiritual weakness is the path for becoming strong in Christ.

Many followers of Jesus lose sight of the continual heart-change that must take place throughout their lives. The tendency is to come to Christ as a broken person, but after a while to revert back to the religious practices of do's and don'ts to measure our status. Have you noticed the tendency of believers to point to the "big" sins of others so that they feel better about their own "little" sins? It's a temptation we must face head on. Sadly, so much of the history of the Church demonstrates how easy it is for Jesus' followers to lose sight of this inside-out transformation.

Why do you think Jesus taught us to ask our Father for his kingdom to come? He knows our hearts. He knows our tendencies. He knows how easy it is for us to slip back into a performance mode of trying to do the right things in our own strength. That is why Jesus taught us to pray for his kingdom to come. We need a regular re-alignment. The kingdom of God, coming in the hearts of his people, causes them to change the way they think and feel and respond. The kingdom of God comes in great power as it changes people from the inside out. Remember from Ezekiel, that the New Covenant promised a heart transplant, not a bypass or a few stints.

No one enters the kingdom of God without being born from above (John 3:1-8; 1 John 3:2, 9, 4:6-7, 5:1, 4, 18-19) and no one lives in the light of the Kingdom without a continual, inner transformation. God wants to give us his Spirit and he is all we need. We need his wisdom and we need his power. We must learn how to ask and keep asking for our Father to give us his power to be strong through his Spirit working in our hearts. As you seek this in your life and in the lives of those you pray for, by asking and continuing to ask, you will experience a new, joy-filled strength within. This is the life abundant that Jesus came to give us.

The inner being vs the old self

In Chapter 7 of the letter to the church in Rome, the apostle Paul was led by the Spirit to explain the internal war that happens in every believer. *So I find it to be a law that when I want to do right, evil lies close at hand. For I delight in the law of God, in my inner being, but I see in my members another law waging war against the law of my mind and making me captive to the law of sin that dwells in my members. Wretched man that I am! Who will deliver me from this body of death?* (Romans 7:21-24) Don't you connect with how Paul felt?

As long as we live in these mortal bodies, we will always struggle with this internal war that rages. Our new heart wants to do what is right and to follow Jesus. However, the body that we inhabit was born in sin and is embedded with sin. In addition to our sin problem, evil forces on the outside try to persuade us to reject Jesus' ways. Notice Paul stated that he delighted in the law of God. In his inner being he loved God's Word and God's ways and wanted to live in full devotion. Going back to Ezekiel's prophecy (page 65), God promised that he would write his laws on our new hearts. But the law of sin was still embedded within Paul's body, as it is still firmly rooted in you and me. We desperately need the power of God to win the daily battles. We know we will win the war, in the end. Jesus has already done that for us. But it's those daily skirmishes and personal struggles against sin and evil that we can win with God's powerful help.

Later in Ephesians, Paul wrote some scary stuff: *We do not wrestle against flesh and blood, but against the rulers, against the authorities, against the cosmic powers over this present darkness, against the spiritual forces of evil in the heavenly places.* (6:12) Yikes! That's terrifying. You may have read Frank Peretti's novels, written in the late 80's and 90's, that portrayed fictionally how these evil forces might work. The first novel was titled after this verse, *This Present Darkness.* Frank helped us to try and comprehend what might be happening in the spirit world around us, but it was scary reading. I'm so glad we can't see what's happening in the unseen world. But we don't need to be afraid. The answer to overcoming their influence was given in v10: *Finally, be strong in the Lord and in the strength of his might. Put on the whole armor of God, that you may be able to stand against the schemes of the devil.* This is a command.

It's not a suggestion or a recommendation. Why? Because we desperately need the strength of his might. Don't be weak. Be strong. Don't try to be strong in yourself. You can't, at least not for very long. Be powerful in the Lord and in the strength of his might.

Have you noticed that when the apostle wrote about the power of God that he used multiple words to describe it? We looked at this trio of power words in the third result of the first Kingdom Come Prayer in Chapter 3 of this book (pages 83-89). Remember that the Spirit of God inspired the writers to use very specific words when they wrote the Bible. He used multiple words for power to help us understand just how much we need this completely unlimited strength of God in our lives. The Spirit's purpose was to envision for us that God's magnificent power is not only what we need, it is what is available to us, as we ask him for it. His Spirit comes along beside us and lives in us to strengthen us to love God with all our heart, soul, mind and might.

Examples of strengthening

For the past couple of years, I have made a concerted effort to gain control over my temper while driving. Do you have that temptation too? Apparently, a lot of drivers do. I have always been reluctant to put a Christian bumper sticker or fish symbol on my car due to my quick temper. What has made this especially challenging for me is that drivers where I live have become significantly more selfish in the past few years. Jesus said that before he returns, the love of people will grow cold. I think I'm witnessing that every day on the roads! It's scary how often I see people run red lights. The recent victories that I've enjoyed have come from asking God to strengthen me in my inner being, so that

I'll stay in control and not take the driving sins of others personally. If someone cuts me off or doesn't use their turn signal, I strive to let it go, by the power of God. My wife and I laugh about it as we sing Queen Elsa's famous chorus (alias Demi Lovato), "*Let it go, let it go…*". I can only let driving infractions go if I am conscious of God's power working in me. I know that on my own, I will get angry in traffic. Every time I try on my own, I fail. When I ask God to give me his power to stay cool, calm and collected, I'm better, much better. I can drive anger-free through Christ who strengthens me! And so can you. Paul experienced the Spirit empowering him whether he had food and shelter or not: *I can do all things through him who strengthens me.* (Philippians 4:13)

We read that the apostle Paul had some kind of debilitating physical problem. He didn't tell us what the specific issue was, he just called it his *thorn in the flesh.* Like any of us would do, Paul pleaded with the Lord to take it away. But Jesus spoke to him and said: "*My grace is sufficient for you, for my power is made perfect in weakness.*" (2 Corinthians 12:9) God's power in our lives doesn't mean every issue will be fixed like we want it to be. On the contrary. The way we often experience the gracious power of God in our lives is when he sustains us through a very difficult time, when we realize we are weak. When we are in those tough times of life, we often cry out to God for his strength. But our Father wants us to learn to ask him for his power more regularly. He wants us to realize that we need his mighty energy working within us each and every day if we're going to live lives that are worthy of our calling. Paul experienced the grace of Jesus as he was strengthened by God's Spirit. As he recognized the limits of his personal strength and relied on God's power, he found that he could overcome anything. And so can you. You can do all things through Christ who strengthens you as you ask the Father to give you his power through his Spirit in your heart and soul.

Stop trying to follow Jesus in your own strength. Stop trying to control your life or overcome temptations by yourself. Accept how weak you really are and enjoy the freedom of depending on the Father to give you the power you need so that Christ is fully formed in you. Until you recognize your weakness to overcome a temptation, like gossip, you won't rely on God's power for victory. Until I began asking God to give me his strength through his Spirit, I lost my temper at other drivers. When I get in the car, if I'll pause a few seconds to remember how easy it is for me to lose my cool, I'll take the time to ask God to give me his strength. That's when I experience the reality of his power being made perfect through my weakness. Having a short fuse behind the wheel is the one weakness I'll go public with. But I can assure you that the power of God to make me more holy is the only reason I remain a faithful follower of the Lord Jesus. The same is true of you, whether you know it yet or not.

Let's now turn to the three results that come from asking the Father to make us mighty by his power through his Spirit in our inner being. As you read about these results, keep in your mind that they all come about through God granting you to be made strong.

Result #1 – So that Christ is at home

The impact in your life of asking your Father to make you strong by his power through his Spirit in your heart of hearts will be: *so that Christ may dwell in your hearts through faith—that you, being rooted and grounded in love.*

(Ephesians 3:17) As mentioned previously, the English translations treat this part of the prayer differently. Some begin a new request in the middle of this sentence, asking for us to be rooted and grounded in love. The English Standard Version emphasizes the link between the clauses and the request. A literal translation of the original is: *that Christ may dwell through faith in your hearts, in love having been rooted and having been grounded.* I don't want to get too picky about the proper translation of this phrase. However, my experience in praying this prayer for many years is that expecting the result of Christ's presence in me by asking for Spiritual strength is more natural to picture in my mind. For the Lord Jesus to be at home in my emotions, desires and dreams, it takes tremendous power from the Spirit working in my soul.

As Jesus is more and more at home in your heart, you will become more and more rooted and grounded in his kind of love. This is a mind-boggling concept. Jesus can dwell in your heart, through your faith, as God empowers you with his Spirit's strength. As you and Jesus become more comfortable with each other, which means you realize that he knows everything, you can't help but be more solidified in his love. Doesn't that make sense?

We've already looked at several Bible passages that teach us about the Spirit living within us. Jesus and his Spirit exist in such unity with the Father that it is absolutely correct to say that Jesus lives in you. In actuality, Jesus is seated with his Father in the heavenlies. But, because he is completely one with the Spirit, even though it is the Spirit who inhabits us, the Bible rightly states that *Christ may dwell in your hearts.* Since the words were inspired by the Spirit as he breathed them out through the various writers, it is actually the Spirit himself who stated that Jesus dwells in our hearts. Have you noticed in the Bible that the Spirit rarely brought attention to himself? He inspired the writers to focus much more on the Father and the Son rather than on himself. He's almost the forgotten member of the Trinity. By the Spirit emphasizing the Father and the Son, we are given one more example of the depth of love and devotion each member of the Trinity has for the others.

The word "to dwell" means to inhabit or to be at home. The opposite of this word means to be a guest or a visitor. There is an ownership issue conveyed. Jesus comes in like he owns the place and has full reign over every room and every closet. A great little book came out in 1986 by RB Munger titled, *My Heart Christ's Home.* It's a best seller and I highly recommend it. Munger takes us through each room in our heart, just like in our homes, to see if Jesus is really welcomed there and comfortable with all that goes on in that particular room. If you picture your heart or mind as a home with multiple rooms and closets, is there a place in your heart's home where Jesus has little influence? For most of us, we have a room or a closet or two where the Lord is kept off limits. Almost subconsciously, we live as if we can hide things from God. Nothing is hidden from his view. Your deepest thoughts and cravings are in vivid HD clarity before him. Therefore, we need the power of God to help us to be able to open those locked doors, to clean out those sin-stained closets and invite Jesus to live there as a permanent resident.

Another way to consider this illustration is to think about Jesus Christ as a guest or a roommate. Could your life be depicted as a home where Jesus is asked to come to dinner on occasion or invited over to hang out and watch the game? If your relationship to God is about going to a church service once a week, then Jesus is more of a guest that comes on Sundays rather than a welcomed roommate. Even for the most faithful followers, thinking about the reality of Jesus' presence in us every moment of every day is difficult to do. It takes the power of the Father, who gives us his strength through his Spirit, to keep us desiring his Son to be a cherished resident rather than an occasional guest.

As you read this, you may be convicted by the Spirit that he doesn't really feel at home in your heart. Are there areas of your life that you don't feel comfortable opening up to Jesus? Confess this sin and begin asking God to empower you so that Jesus can take up residence in your heart. Ask the Father, according to the riches of his glory, to give you the power to open that locked room so you can work together to clean it out. You need the power of God to help you remove the things that you don't want Jesus to see. You can do this through Christ who is your strength.

One more thing. You can't remove the junk from a room and it be warm and cozy. You have to refurnish it. As we read earlier, we are to take off the old and put on the new. By the power of God, you can replace sinful habits with righteous actions. I'm not only learning to not get angry at other drivers, I'm learning how to be a gracious driver. Looking at porn isn't solved by stopping the sin. A positive action must replace the negative one. Reading the Bible, listening to righteous music, reading Christian novels or volunteering your time are all positive ways to replace the sin of looking at porn. Gossiping has to be replaced with speaking the truth in love, by the power of God. Coveting is conquered when it is replaced with a sense of thankfulness and appreciation for what the Lord has given you, and that includes your stuff, your abilities, your circumstances and your relationships. All of this is possible by the strength our Father wants to give us as we ask him so that Jesus can inhabit our heart's home.

He dwells within by faith

Let's now focus on two words in this statement that are pivotal: *through faith.* The first result of asking the Father to give you his power is that Jesus dwells in your heart through your faith in him. You are empowered by God to believe that Jesus lives in your heart, by his Spirit. Our belief isn't based on feelings or emotions we conjure up. Our faith is based on fact. God says unequivocally that he and the Son live within each believer through the Spirit. Again, we need to go back to the promise of the New Covenant. Hundreds of years before Jesus came to earth, God promised that he would give his people a new spirit and a new heart. When you came to believe in Jesus as the Son of God who paid your ransom price, you were given his Spirit to live within you for the rest of your life. Jesus declared to his disciples on that Holy Thursday night that the New Covenant was about to be ratified: "*If you love me, you will keep my commandments. And I will ask the Father, and he will give you another Helper, to be with you forever, even the Spirit of truth, whom the world cannot receive, because it neither sees him nor knows him. You know him, for he dwells with you and will be in you.*" (John 14:15-17)

Notice closely Jesus' words. He stated that the Helper, the Holy Spirit, was *with* them. How did that work? Because Jesus lived with them he could also say the Spirit lived with them. But something wonderful is about to happen. The age of the New Covenant is about to be begin. That's why Jesus said in the next phrase that the Helper, a very descriptive name for the Spirit, will be *in* you. Those two unique prepositions represent an amazing new era for mankind. Jesus, Emmanuel, God with us, is about to be God *in* us. Jesus' promise became reality when the Spirit first inhabited the 120 believers on the day of Pentecost in Acts Chapter 2.

Because God said so

However, our experience is that most of the time, you have no proof at all that Jesus' Spirit is living in you. You don't feel like he is there. There's no outward sign. There's no inward sensation. Most of the time, the only way that you know the Spirit is in you is because God said he is. Jesus promised you that he is there and that there is nothing in this world or the spirit world that can separate you from him: *For I am sure that neither death nor life, nor angels nor rulers, nor things present nor things to come, nor powers, nor height nor depth, nor anything else in all creation, will be able to separate us from the love of God in Christ Jesus our Lord.* (Romans 8:38-39) Once he comes to live in you, he will never leave you or vacate the premises. Jesus has promised you and me that he is with us every step of the way, regardless of how we feel. Faith can't be based on feelings.

Are there times when you feel his presence? Sure. You know that's true. Are there times when others see the power of God working in and through you. Absolutely. But most of the time, it's a matter of faith. What exactly is faith in Jesus? *Now faith is the assurance of things hoped for, the conviction of things not seen.* (Hebrews 11:1) Faith is the certainty that everything God has told us in his Bible is true. Faith convicts us that even though we can't see the presence of Jesus living in us through his Spirit, he is there. What do you need to do when your faith is wobbling and you're struggling with believing that Jesus is at home in your life? Ask your Father to give you his power. Ask him once and ask him again and ask him each day and ask him throughout the day. He will empower you so that your faith gets stronger and Jesus becomes your trusted roommate rather than an occasional dinner guest.

Love, rooted and grounded

The result of Christ taking up permanent residency in your heart is that Jesus' love will be more and more the basis and foundation of your life. There are two descriptive illustrations in this prayer's phrase: *being rooted and grounded in love.* On the one hand, you will become rooted like a huge oak tree. No matter how much the winds of hardships blow, your love will hold fast because your roots go down deep in the power of God. Jesus' love in your life can also be depicted as the strong foundation of a well-built building. Picture a large building whose foundation reaches deep into the earth so that it can weather the strongest tornado or Category 5 hurricane.

Your faith in Jesus' presence in you is how his love gets rooted and grounded in your life. It is the gift of God's power that brings this about as you ask him to strengthen your heart. As you are empowered by the Spirit, you can open up more honestly and openly to Jesus, then your firm position will be steadfastly established in Christ Jesus' kind of love.

The kind of love that we're being rooted and grounded in has three dimensions. It is the steadfast love that Jesus has for us as his brothers and sisters. It is also the love that we have for Jesus, his Father and the Spirit.

And it is the love that we believers have for one another. The context of this prayer, and the entire letter to the church in Ephesus, spells out all three dimensions of Jesus' love.

God strengthening you in your inner being means Jesus will be more at home in your heart. You will be more aware of his constant presence. You will no longer want to hide things from him (as if you could hide anything from Jesus). You will stop trying to pretend he doesn't know what you're up to. As you get more comfortable with the Spirit's power in his presence, you will love the Lord with greater devotion. You will find it easier to confess your daily sins to him – which you'll recall from The Followers' Prayer is the fourth part of our praying (pages 42-45). You will also begin to understand how great his love is for you. And most importantly, you will begin to love people in your church, as well as all other believers, with more consistency. That's what it means to be rooted and grounded in agape love. And this rooting and grounding comes about as we ask the Father to strengthen us.

Jesus' kind of love

What is agape love? Jesus took an ordinary Greek word and exploded it into the rich reality of his kingdom. "Agape" was an ancient word that was different from the more popular words used in those days for romantic love and brotherly love. It was used primarily to describe the Greek gods. In Greek mythology, agape was the word used for the love that the gods chose to give to certain people, especially rulers and generals. Jesus took this word and gave it new power and a much fuller meaning. The forgiveness of sins that he purchased releases a whole new kind of love, agape love, that overflows, fills and directs all of life, thoughts and actions. We have no English word like it. The closest is altruism. How often do you hear that word used? Me neither.

I love fried chicken. I don't eat it as often as I used to because so many people say that it isn't healthy. I love the phrase, "Eat Mor Chikin"! I also love football. I'm writing this in the fall, which is the pinnacle of football season, both college and professional. Football season is the best time of the year, at least in my mind it is. I love the beach and the mountains. I love my wife, Tammy, and I love the Lord Jesus. Now how in the world can one word adequately express my feelings for fried chicken, football, my wife and my Lord?

Agape love is how Jesus explained his Father's mercy for us: "*For God so loved* (agape-d) *the world, that he gave his only Son, that whoever believes in him should not perish but have eternal life. For God did not send his Son into the world to condemn the world, but in order that the world might be saved through him.* (John 3:16-17) God agape loved us before we ever returned that love. He agape loves us with such magnitude that we could never adequately reciprocate it. That is the basis of agape love – it doesn't require reciprocation. It's not a tit for tat that if you love me I'll love you back. Agape love has a price. Agape love always costs the giver. Agape love is a selfless love that focuses completely on the receiver, not the giver. A stunning example of agape love happened when the Roman soldiers were impaling Jesus to the cross: "*Father, forgive them, for they don't know what they are doing.*" (Luke23:34 - NLT) Isn't it true that we are often hurt by people who don't really know what they are doing? Stop and think about that question before continuing.

The agape love that the first believers held for one

another turned Jerusalem upside down. The power of God was so strong in them that they sold their personal possessions to provide food and shelter for other believers who were in need. (Acts 2:42-47 and 4:32-37) Agape love was so tangible in that church that no one was left out. The first church experienced incredible agape love and it remains the model for every church today. Jesus' command to agape love one another was lived out every day and in every tangible way in that first church in Jerusalem. It was also the first mega-church with estimates of 30,000 Jewish believers. The first church grew and flourished because of the power of God to strengthen his people to agape love one another.

I wonder if the greatest challenge you face is the same one that I struggle with – agape loving every other believer the same way that Jesus agape loves them. People can be so annoying. They can be so different in their thinking. People, especially God's people, seem to have so many little quirks. Many of them just seem downright weird. And some personalities rub me the wrong way. I sometimes find it easier to love those who are far from God than the saints who are adopted into the family with me. Can you relate?

Freely receive, freely give

Jesus made it crystal clear: *This is my commandment, that you love one another as I have loved you.* (John 15:12) The old apostle John hammered this commandment in all of his writings. It couldn't be any clearer. Our highest responsibility in the kingdom of God is to agape love all of those God has called into his kingdom, every last one of them, no matter what. But it is really hard to do. We know that all too well. What is needed is a constant plea to God to empower us so that we can keep Christ at home in our hearts and be rock-solid in our agape love for him and for all of his people.

When that church member you don't particularly care for says or does something that grates against your nerves, it is time to cry out to the Father for his power so that you can agape love them. Realize too that your relationship with another believer is never one-on-one. Christ is always there. He lives in you and the other believer through his Spirit. The more I remind myself of this truth, especially when I'm ticked off by another believer, it really helps. I find that asking the Father to grant me to be strengthened helps me to live in the consciousness of his presence which gives me more incentive to agape love like he does. We are all in desperate need of the Father to strengthen us so that we can take direct control of our thinking, to turn it to agape love.

How patient has the Father been with you to this point in your life? His grace is truly amazing. We so rarely beg him to make us strong through his Spirit. How much more peace could you enjoy if you were truly comfortable with Jesus knowing everything you're thinking? This is your Father's desire for you. He wants you to become at home with the influence of the Holy Spirit in you so that the center of your being is rooted and grounded in the agape love of Christ. Being empowered by the Spirit means we will think and act more like Jesus thought and acted. God is forming Christ in you. You probably won't heal a blind person like he did, but you will be able to agape love someone who rejects you, or is unfaithful or rude to you.

When Jesus is at home in our thoughts and emotions, we can be very open and honest with our Father. The more honest we are, the deeper our relationship becomes. Isn't that true in all of your relationships with people? Sure it is, and it's the same way with your Father in the heavens. Anytime you are brutally honest with yourself about the things that really matter in life, you will realize your need for God's power. Maybe I should reword that. You will realize your desire for God's power. God's power is what you will begin to want more than anything, because of the amazing results his power brings to your heart. The first result is Christ's welcomed residency that bases your life in agape love.

Got Christ inside? Ask your Father, according to the vast treasures of his magnificent splendor, to give you his mighty power through his Spirit in your inner self so that your faith in Jesus' abiding presence makes you agape love like he does.

Result #2 – So that you understand Christ's love

So that you *may have strength to comprehend with all the saints what is the breadth and length and height and depth, and to know the love of Christ that surpasses knowledge.* This is the second result of the Father giving his power to his children. They will have the power that's needed to understand the full volume of the agape love of Jesus. This result takes our understanding of the agape love of Jesus to new heights. Let's dive into what this looks like in our lives.

Do you understand the dimensions of Christ's love? Of course not, not fully. So let us be diligent to ask the Father to grant us to be strengthened by his power through his Spirit in our inner self, being rooted and grounded in agape love. Stop and ponder what the Spirit meant when he led Paul to write such a statement - *the breadth and length and height and depth, and to know the love of Christ that surpasses knowledge.* What image comes to mind when you think about how broad and long and high and deep the love of Jesus is? What is the Spirit trying to help us see?

The Spirit moved Paul to describe the fullness of Jesus' love as having four dimensions. What in the world is 4D? It's beyond our world. The fullness of Jesus' love is so great that it is in an entirely different realm from our 3D world. Can you understand it fully? Not yct. Thc cross is the proof of the full volume of Jesus' love for his Father, his love for us and the Father's love for the world. *Therefore be imitators of God, as beloved children. And walk in love, as Christ loved us and gave himself up for us, a fragrant offering and sacrifice to God.* (Ephesians 5:1-2) In giving up his holy life as the sacrifice and atonement for our sins, Jesus demonstrated his sacrificial love for his people, his devoted love for his Father and the Father's selfless love for rebellious people. To have the power to comprehend the magnitude and dimensions of the love of Jesus, we must consider how broad and long and high and deep his sacrifice was for us.

The love of Jesus and his willingness to be made sin on our behalf has no limits. He took on your sins and my sins and was punished by his Father for our sin crimes. His love reaches out widely to every person who is willing to accept it. There is no one so evil that the love of Jesus can't penetrate his or her heart. Jesus suffered from the breadth and length and height and depth of the sins of mankind – every sin imaginable. His love is so broad that it surpasses all of those sins. The volume of his love is able to contain and to atone for all of the sins of mankind. There is no sin that can't be covered over, except the sin of rejecting his forgiveness. You probably know the illustration parents sometimes use – stretching their arms as wide as possible and saying, "I love you this much!" That's the breadth of Jesus' love. He stretched his arms as widely as he could, and allowed Roman soldiers to impale them to a cross beam to demonstrate his love for you, me and his Father.

Jesus' love is also long. We know the length of his love because we have all made him wait, possibly for years and years, before we confessed our sins and received his love. His waiting is not over once we finally accept his love and receive him as our Lord. He will continue to show you the length of his love as he waits for you to turn from that reoccurring sin or to serve where he's been trying to get you to go. Jesus will have to wait, maybe a long time, for you to forgive someone who owes you. His love for us is so very long.

His love for us is high enough to overcome every rejection there is, because his love is the same as his Father's love. His Father gave his best to mankind so the Son does the same. The height of the love of Jesus stretches the expanse of the universe. There is no limit. And the depth of Jesus' love knows all of your deepest secrets, the things you wouldn't dare tell your wife or husband or even closest friend. He knows all of your thoughts and those dreams that wake you up in a cold sweat and he loves you anyway. The Lamb of God loves you in spite of all of the sin you carry within. He loves you even when you deny your love for him and act like you don't belong to him. This is the breadth, the length, the height and the depth of the love of God which is in Christ Jesus our Lord. This is agape love. The praise band, Jesus Culture, wrote a powerful song reminding us of his love titled, "One Thing Remains". It opens with:

> Higher than the mountains that I face
> Stronger than the power of the grave

Constant through the trial and the change
This one thing remains, this one thing remains
Your love never fails, it never gives up
It never runs out on me

How will we ever have the strength to understand the full volume of the love of Jesus? Only as we keep asking our Father, according to the riches of his glory, to grant us to be empowered with his power through his Spirit deep within our souls. Our Father wants us to know his Son's love that, oddly enough, is actually beyond knowing. What in the world does that mean?

Christ's love surpasses knowledge because humans can never completely understand the full extent of the Son's love, at least not on this side of eternity. When we are with him, in his visible presence, we will experience the fullness of his love and glory. From the way Jesus prayed in John 17, it sounds like he can't wait to show us the full extent of his love in his glory. But human eyes and hearts can't absorb it. Only when he has made us immortal can we take in the vastness of his love. But until that day comes, we must ask and keep asking our Father to empower us.

With all the saints

The final part of this second result shows us how important the local church is to us and to Christ. Again, the result is that you: *may have strength to comprehend with all the saints what is the breadth and length and height and depth, and to know the love of Christ that surpasses knowledge.* We have yet to consider the phrase, *all the saints.* Remember this is a letter to the church in the city of Ephesus. Back in those days, there was only one church in each city.

The love of Christ is to be understood by all believers,

the saints. Paul didn't pray, and neither should we, that only certain individuals would be strengthened by God to be strong enough to comprehend Christ's love. He prayed that everyone in that church would experience his gigantic agape love. He goes on to explain in Ephesians 4 that the church is paramount in God's rescue mission. The only way an individual believer can grow in their faith, live in a way that is worthy of their calling, and comprehend the love of Jesus is through their belonging to a local church. You can't experience the empowerment of God to know the fullness of Jesus' love if you are not involved with and committed to a local church. The church is Jesus' bride. The church is what Jesus is building. We can only know the fullness of his agape love for us by experiencing it with other followers who are demonstrating it to us and with us.

The love of Jesus is both his love for his Father and his love for his people. We've already looked at his highest command, that we are to emulate his love for his people. Because we are all called the beloved, we are to agape love each other in the same way that Jesus loves us. He loves us when we don't love him back. So agape love is never conditional. It doesn't wait until the person in your home group asks for forgiveness. Agape love extends forgiveness before it is ever deserved, which is the love of Christ that the Father wants us to know and experience. If it is beyond knowing, that means it must be understood and experienced. Agape love goes beyond your knowledge of another believer's faults, sins and imperfections. Despite all that you know about that person and the terrible things they've done, you are called to agape love them because Jesus loves them unconditionally. You can only do that through the power of God working in you. But you can do it. You can love the most unloving believer through the power of experiencing the full volume of the love of Jesus.

How are things going in your church? Is there strife? Are there broken relationships? Any squabbling on the elder or deacon teams? What should you do when there is? Pray like crazy! Ask your Father in the heavens that according to the riches of his glory he will empower everyone in your church with strength through his Spirit, so that everyone is rooted and grounded in agape love. Then your church can begin to have the strength to understand how Jesus' love is so much bigger than their silly differences like the type of music that is played, the length of the sermons, how announcements are handled or how frequently you celebrate the Lord's Supper.

Pastors, church leaders, and worship directors, you must pray this way! Praying regularly and passionately these Kingdom Come Prayers for your entire church family is probably the best thing you can do for them. If Paul and his team never stopped praying this way for all the churches of their day, you certainly are called by God to do the same for the one church you lead. In one of the churches I was privileged to pastor, the elders and I were led by the Spirit to list all the members of our church according to the days of the week. We took the entire membership and divided them among the 7 days of the week so we could pray for each person and each family using the Kingdom Come Prayers.

Do you work with a believer from another church? Do they get on your nerves? Do you get on their last nerve? Does that other church have some weird traditions or practices? How is Jesus' church manifested at your place of employment, your school and in your town or city? This prayer is for all believers in all the local churches. Imagine the impact if outsiders in your town saw churches coming together in the love of Jesus? Imagine the impact at your work if all the other employees saw you and every other believer agape loving each other every day? Imagine how your school would change if all the believers (students, faculty and staff) consistently agape loved each other in the same way that Jesus loves. Isn't it time for an Agape Love Revolution in your church, at your office, at your school and in your town?

Our Father wants all of his children to be so connected with the indwelling Holy Spirit that the love of Jesus for us, our love for him and our love for one another will saturate every desire and every action. Is it possible? It is by asking according to God's will!

Result #3 – So that you will be filled

The prayer crescendos into an almost inconceivable truth in the final result: *that you may be filled with all the fullness of God.* Yep, you need to read that one again. This is God's intended outcome of all that has been requested in this prayer. This is the goal of salvation for our lives on earth – that Christ is fully formed in us. Really? A person can be filled with all of God's fullness? Not really. Jesus was, of course. Jesus was the fullness of God's deity in human form. And you and I certainly aren't Jesus. So what does this crescendo mean for us?

The words "filled" and "fullness" come from how Paul's peers would describe a full ship. When all of the sailors, the rowers, the soldiers, the supplies and the cargo were on board, the ship was then "full". So for us, it's the picture of a plane with all the crew members, all the passengers, all the luggage and any freight; the tanks are full of fuel and the galley is full of snacks and drinks - then the plane is full.

The fullness of God is the totality of his attributes that can be given to his people, like the fruit of the Spirit – love, joy, peace, patience, kindness, goodness, faithfulness, gentleness and self-control. Not included in this list of attributes is God's wisdom, knowledge and power. Since the fullness of God was in the man Jesus Christ, we can look to Jesus to understand God's goal for his people in this process of continual transformation. He wants the nature of his Son fully formed within us so that we are mature in Christ.

But no person could possibly contain the fullness of all that God is. The fullness of God is how he makes his power and his presence visible to the world. As we experience God doing in us and through us what we could never do on our own, we are being filled with his grace. But his fullness is not for individuals. The fullness of God is experienced in his local churches, among the gathered saints who are learning and experiencing the full volume of the love of Christ.

We tend to read this prayer as if it is meant for us as individual believers. Remember, first and foremost this letter and the prayer within it are for his gathered believers, Christ's church. To be filled with God's fullness is to be filled up to all the measure of God's fullness that is on display in the church. It is God's power and love that he wants to pour out on his people. This is more easily understood as we continue reading in Ephesians. From this prayer, Paul is led to write about why the church exists and how it is intended to work. In Ephesians 4, he described a unified group of followers of Jesus who are all doing their part, according to their Spiritual giftedness, building each other up: *until we all attain to the unity of the faith and of the knowledge of the Son of God, to mature manhood, to the measure of the stature of the fullness of Christ.* (4:13)

One person can not have the fullness of God. One person can't display all of the attributes of Jesus' nature. The diversity of how God gives individuals Spiritual gifts is evidence of our dependence on one another. God's fullness is manifested through his church as each person is learning how to be who God has rebirthed them to be and serving accordingly. It takes the whole church together, with all of its diversities, gifts, talents, passions and experiences to demonstrate the fullness of Jesus Christ.

Growing up together

The verses that follow the prayer tell us how this happens: *Rather, speaking the truth in love, we are to grow up in every way into him who is the head, into Christ, from whom the whole body, joined and held together by every joint with which it is equipped, when each part is working properly, makes the body grow so that it builds itself up in love.* (4:15-16) Don't miss the key. Each part is working properly. That means that each member of your church is growing together in their knowledge of God and in his power working within them (another clear reason why the leaders of a church must pray diligently for each person who calls the church home). If each person is working properly, then they are serving in the area where they can make the greatest contribution to the whole. It does not mean Alicia gets to sing on the Praise Team even though she's not a good singer. It definitely does not mean David gets to teach when he's the only person in the church who thinks he's a good teacher. It does mean that we speak the truth about life and Christ in agape love to one another. As the church is firing on all cylinders, everyone gets built up in love and grows into a mature, fully grown-up Jesus.

You know as well as I do that the problem with most churches is you and me! The Me Monster is alive and well within most of our churches today. We typically find a church that suits our style, with a pastor that we like, a building that is suitable and music that we are comfortable with. This attitude is depicted in a 2006 country by Josh Turner, called "Me and God". The title conveys our sentiment so well. Josh, I don't mean to slam your song writing. You do have some excellent lyrics in the song that describes a close relationship with the Father, which is what these prayers are to accomplish. But the idea of life being all about just me and my relationship with God is prevalent in so many song lyrics. And that's the problem with most of us. I'm too much about me.

When you read earlier in this book that the Epistles were primarily written to local churches, were you surprised? Have you ever thought about the fact that these letters were written to the gathered local church rather than to individuals. Our typical individualistic mindset drives us to think of them as very personal letters. They have even been called love letters to us, as if God were writing just to you. The language throughout the letters, and throughout both of these Kingdom Come Prayers in Ephesians, is in plural form. You can read every "you" as "y'all" if you're from the south, or "you guys" if your heritage is more northern. That makes sense because you can't picture Paul and his team praying for some of the believers and not for others.

The prayer request here is that everyone in the church in Ephesus will be empowered by God's Spirit so that Christ can be at home in all of their hearts so that they can comprehend together the vastness of his love, experiencing it in all its fullness so as a group they can be filled with all of God's fullness. God wants to receive glory through the church's expression of his fullness as each person grows accordingly, at their own pace. Underline "at their own pace"!

It's critical for each of us to ask if we are working properly for our church. Are you doing what God has called and is equipping you to do? Also, are you doing anything to stunt the growth of your church? Are you gossiping, complaining, being greedy, arguing, coveting, withholding your money or your time? If so, know that you are living as the dead person that you were. You were dead to God until he chose to give you new life. Why in the world would you choose to live like you were still dead, rather than being alive in Christ?

Stop thinking of "going to church" and what you can get out of it. Take on God's perspective of "being the church" and what you can pour into it. As you learn to persistently ask God to grant you, and everybody else in your small group or church, to be strengthened with power through his Spirit in your inner being, you will learn to treasure each other better. The fullness of God will be on vivid display for everyone in the church to enjoy and for outsiders to witness. As you learn of the full volume of the love of Christ, your heart's eyes will be enlightened and your spirit will be empowered to want to show that same love to every other follower of Jesus. This love will then go way beyond what you all know about each other so that you all experience agape love as God intended.

The real test of whether Jesus is becoming more of a welcomed resident in your heart is whether you are growing in your agape love for him and for all other believers. If you're not experiencing this growth, then pray like crazy this Kingdom Come Prayer. Are your children struggling in their relationship with God? Keep asking the Father to strengthen them with his Spirit, according to the glory of his riches. As you continue to ask the Father, you will see these three very profound results coming about. This is God's will for you and for those you are praying for and for your church as a whole. God's ultimate desire is for each of his local churches to be filled with all of his attributes. That's what will give him the most glory. This is his kingdom coming to earth.

But is all of this really possible? The prayer is so magnificent and so different from how we typically pray. Can a local church really be filled with God's fullness like this? Can believers really be so empowered by God that Jesus is at home in our hearts and we are experiencing more and more of his limitless love?

The breath-taking blessing

Now to him who is able to do far more abundantly than all that we ask or think, according to the power at work within us, to him be glory in the church and in Christ Jesus throughout all generations, forever and ever. Amen. (Ephesians 3:20-21) God knew full well that you and I would wonder if this prayer could become reality. He knows that we doubt. We don't doubt whether he can or wants to bring these changes about. We doubt whether he will do it through us or in our church. "I know God can, but can he really do it in me, in us?" That's why the Spirit led Paul into this stunning promise and blessing in the middle of his letter. By the way, that's not where you are supposed to put benedictions (a fancy word for blessings). Why is it in Chapter 3 rather than at the end of Chapter 6? Because our loving Father knew we needed this incredibly inspiring truth to follow such a grandiose prayer.

*Now to him who is able…*You are not able. You can't do any of these things. You are not able to empower yourself or live grounded in agape love or grasp the full volume of the love of Jesus. God is able. He is so able that he has the ability to do infinitely more than what is even in this prayer. Each time you pray to the Father, he is able to far surpass what you prayed and even what you weren't brave enough to pray. How is he able to do what we ask and even the unthinkable?

He is able because of the power at work within us. Notice it's "us" and not "me" or "you". God is able to do all of these amazing things through his power that is working in and through all of his people gathered together in his church. If you weren't sure whether this was all about God working through his church, just read what follows that phrase: *to him be glory in the church and in Christ Jesus throughout all generations, forever and ever. Amen.* God wants to be glorified in his churches, by what they are doing and how they are demonstrating the agape love of Jesus. To be glorified means that he is getting all of the credit for all of the good that is taking place. People see the good things a church is doing and they give God all the praise.

Don't ever forget that God is able. He is able to do more amazing things than you can possibly comprehend. He is able to do these things because he is giving his churches his power through his Spirit, grounding and rooting his people in agape love. His desire is for his people to experience the same kind of love for one another that the Father, Son and Spirit have for each other.

Paul was inspired to wrap up the letter with a very cool illustration in Chapter 6. Picture the apostle locked in a room with a Roman guard, in sort of a minimum security prison. Paul has been given the freedom to write and as he writes, picture the soldier falling asleep. Paul glances up as the guard snores away and is struck with a visual that his audience could identify with. The guard is laying fast asleep decked out in his full armor: helmet, breastplate, belt, boots, shield and sword. Paul gets an image. As the soldier stands firm in battle, so the believer should stand firm in their faith as they battle against all kinds of evil, from without and within. We previously considered his admonition in 6:10 to *be strong in the Lord and in the strength of his might.* Paul compared the soldier's belt to the truth, his breastplate as righteousness, shoes as readiness to take the good news to others, a shield as our faith, the helmet as our salvation and the sword as God's Word. He wrote: *and take the helmet of salvation, and the sword of the Spirit, which is the word of God, praying at all times in the Spirit, with all prayers and supplication.* (6:17-18a)

The sword of the Spirit is the Word of God. With this sword, the Word of God, we are instructed to pray at all times, through the Spirit's help, with all kinds of requests and petitions. Praying the Kingdom Come Prayers is how we fight against everything that comes against us and those we love. Praying the very words of God in all kinds of situations and circumstances is his will for us. That is why Jesus said that if we remain in him and his words remain in us, we can ask for whatever we want and the Father will answer our request. That is an almost shocking truth. The key is that as we are asking from the very words of Jesus, we are obviously asking according to his heart, which is his will. That is why we can have rock solid confidence as we ask our Father to work according to the Kingdom Come Prayers because they are his words; they are his will. But we must be persistent. The key is to ask God for what he wants to give you. He wants to give you his power, through his Spirit in your inner being. He wants to do that with everyone in your family, your small group and your entire church. Look at how Paul concluded this passage: *To that end keep alert with all perseverance, making supplication for all the saints.* (6:18b)

Do you see how Paul's letters so completely parallel Jesus' teachings? As Jesus instructed us not to lose heart but to keep praying with perseverance, Paul encouraged us to do the exact same thing. Paul explained what Jesus taught because it was the Spirit of Jesus who gave Paul the understanding and the clarity. It was also the Spirit of Jesus who gave Paul the passion and desire to pray continuously for the saints, making all kinds of requests for them to have the Spirit's wisdom and power. He wants to give you and me the same passion and desire. He wants us to intercede for all of the saints in our circle of influence, to regularly pray these Kingdom Come Prayers. "All prayers and supplications" also includes the things we naturally ask God to provide: safety, healing, protection, provisions, etc.

May this reality fuel your desire to pray passionately and persistently for what God wants to give you, your family members, your friends and your church. And *to him be glory in the church and in Christ Jesus throughout all generations, forever and ever. Amen.* Amen means "may it be"; for our day and time it might best be translated, "Yes!"

Small Group Questions

1. If you could be given strength by God right now, in what area of your life would you want his power? How might his power in you change the way you think and act?

2. Read the passages in Ephesians that describe God's power and discuss what stands out to you. 1:19-23; 3:7, 16, 18, 20; 6:10

3. From 3:17, discuss how God making you strong sets up Christ to be more at home in your heart. What would it look like for you to be more comfortable with Jesus? Is he currently more of a roommate or a guest?

4. Read 3:18-19a and discuss what mental image comes to your mind. How can we better understand the full volume of Christ's love? What are some ways you can remind yourself of his love throughout the day?

5. Read the section "Growing up together" beginning on page 128, and discuss what your commitment to your local church should look like. What is your commitment as a small group?

Close your time together by praying through this prayer as a group

Kingdom Come Prayer #2

Ephesians 3:16-19

THE REQUEST

Dear Father in the heavens, I ask that out of your glorious riches, you will grant me to be strengthened with your power, through your Spirit, in the core of my being…

1st Result

so that Jesus will be more at home in my heart through faith, being rooted and grounded in agape love…

2nd Result

so that I'll have strength to understand, with all fellow believers, how wide and high and long and deep Jesus' love is, experiencing it beyond just knowledge…

3rd Result

so that together, we might be filled with all of your fullness.

Chapter 5 - Kingdom Come Prayer #3 Agape Love

And it is my prayer that your love may abound more and more, with knowledge and all discernment, so that you may approve what is excellent, and so be pure and blameless for the day of Christ, filled with the fruit of righteousness that comes through Jesus Christ, to the glory and praise of God. (Philippians 1:9-11)

How do you know which of the Kingdom Come Prayers to pray? This third prayer helps us with that answer in a couple of ways. Knowing the context of each of the prayers is key. Learning certain things about each church as you read the specific letters will increase your understanding of the context. Each church had its unique set of circumstances and challenges, just like every church in existence today. They all had their own traits and each had a unique relationship with Paul. For an even fuller understanding of each of the Epistles, read how that specific church came about in Acts. For example, we learn from Acts 16:6-10 of the unique way that the Spirit of Jesus led Paul and his team to the region of Macedonia, where Philippi is located. The history of the birth of the Philippian church is captured in this same chapter. Paul was not able to remain in Philippi very long. In contrast, he spent three years with the church in Ephesus. (Acts 20:31) Knowing these details will help you to better understand each of the prayers.

Did you notice how different the Philippian prayer is compared to the two in Ephesians? Even though Paul knew the church members in Ephesus better than he did those in Philippi, he had a unique affection for the Philippian believers. He wrote: *For God is my witness, how I yearn for you all with the affection of Jesus Christ.* (1:8) Paul wrote repeatedly in this letter of the joy they brought to his heart, because they were living out their faith so boldly. To the Ephesian church, Paul explained rich doctrinal truths that led to strong admonishments and cautions about living out their faith in righteous behavior. To the Philippians, the apostle focused more on encouragement and praise as he inspired them to keep growing in their faith.

Different requests for different churches

The Philippian letter reveals a church that is healthy and strong in their faith. Paul thanked them for their *partnership in the gospel* (1:5) and felt deeply about them because they were *partners* (1:7 HCSB) as they gave generously to meet Paul's needs (4:10-16). The church also prayed regularly for Paul and his team (1:19). The letter highlights their obedience (2:12) and maturity (3:15). But it was their generosity that was fueled by their agape love that stood out the most.

In his second letter to the church in Corinth, Paul revealed the true heart of the Philippian church. He used their selfless generosity to inspire the believers in Corinth.

> *We want you to know, brothers, about the grace of God that has been given among the churches of Macedonia, for in a severe test of affliction, their abundance of joy and their extreme poverty have overflowed in a wealth of generosity on their part. For they gave according to their means, of their own accord, begging us earnestly for the favor of taking part in the relief of the saints – and this, not as we expected, but they gave themselves first to the Lord and then by the will of God to us.* (2 Corinthians 8:1-5)

There were three churches in the Macedonian region: the Philippian church as well as the churches in Thessalonica and Berea. When you read the two Thessalonian letters, you will see how similar they were to the believers in Philippi. But it was this Philippian church that is most praised for their sacrificial generosity.

When was the last time you heard of a church begging to give money to help out believers, especially believers in another country? The collection was for the churches in Israel that were suffering under a severe draught. The believers in these three churches not only gave generously; they gave out of their own poverty. They weren't just poor; they were extremely poor. The Philippian church apparently led the way. Giving like that definitely comes from a heart for God and for his people. This is agape love in action. Paul went on in the Corinthian letter to state that generous giving is the litmus test of proof that agape love is genuine. (2 Corinthians 8:8, 24)

What can we learn from this church? The prayer request in Philippians 1:9 seems much more suited for believers who are similar to the believers in Philippi. This prayer seems more pertinent for followers of Jesus who are a little further down the tracks. They were by no means perfect and they certainly had not "arrived". But their agape love was sacrificial and tangible; it was a love that was willing to deliberately sacrifice to serve others.

The unique thing about agape love is that it always costs the giver. When agape love is genuine it comes with a price. It will cost you time, mental energy, emotional strength, money, patience and tears. Doesn't it make sense that Paul would pray for those who were tangibly demonstrating their agape love that their love would increase even more? This doesn't mean that you shouldn't pray this way for a brand new believer or someone who is struggling in their faith. It simply makes more sense to pray this way regularly for the person who is following Jesus and striving to honor him.

A few paragraphs after the prayer, Paul wrote: *Therefore, my beloved, as you have always obeyed, so now, not only as in my presence but much more in my absence, work out your own salvation with fear and trembling, for it is God who works in you, both to will and to work for his good pleasure.* (2:12-13) "Beloved" means: the ones who are agape loved. Why does Paul feel this way about them? They are striving to obey all of Jesus' teachings because of their agape love for the Lord. Can't you hear Paul cheering them on as they are seeking to serve Jesus and his people? Therefore, he reminded them that it was God himself who was working in them to give them the desire to love and obey. And it was God himself who was working in them to give them the strength to do the things their faith was leading them to do. Is this descriptive of you? Do you know believers who would have fit in perfectly at the Philippian Community Church? Maybe this prayer in Philippians 1:9-11 is a more strategic request for those who are more mature in their faith. As we unpack this prayer, it will hopefully become clearer why this is likely the case.

THE REQUEST – For love to abound

Like the prayers in Ephesians, this prayer has one request with multiple results. The request is: *And it is my prayer that your love may abound more and more, with knowledge and all discernment.* Paul continually asked that God would make their love abound. It could not happen without his direct involvement. It's evident, from the rest of this letter and all of his other letters, that every Christ-follower is desperately dependent on God.

Our heavenly Father wants us to ask him to make our agape love abound more and more. If agape love is flourishing more and more, then it's already present and active, just like it was in the believers in Philippi. Their agape love inspired them to give extravagantly. The way it is worded in 2 Corinthians 8:1-5, it almost sounds like they gave until they barely had anything left for themselves. Their agape love was already overflowing. So Paul prayed that it would overflow even more and even more beyond that. His vision was that their agape love would continue to increase in devotion to the Lord and to his people. This prayer request is for agape love to grow and overflow continuously, never letting up.

Wouldn't it be cool if your gas tank could do that? You start out with half a tank but the more you drive, the fuller it gets. As you continue driving, it just keeps getting more and more full. You are using gas to drive, but your tank is being replenished with even more than your car is consuming. That's what God wants to do within our hearts with his agape love.

Whose love?

It seems like the request should be for God to make *his* love increase and abound in us. Should it really be *our* agape love that's increasing? Yes! The Spirit's inspired words tell us to pray for *our* agape love to abound and overflow. Why "our" love?

God is love (1 John 4:8). He doesn't have love, it is who he is. The only agape love that you and I have in us is from God. As his born-from-above children, we have been regenerated and given a new heart of agape love. Since the Spirit is in us, agape love is in us. John wrote that we have God's very seed in us. (1 John 3:9) Since we are called to imitate God, we are called to agape love like he does. It is our highest value and the most distinct quality of a follower of Jesus Christ. At least, it's supposed to be our most distinguishing characteristic. Jesus said to his disciples on that Holy Thursday night: "*A new commandment I give to you, that you love* (agape) *one another: just as I have loved* (agape'd) *you, you also are to love* (agape) *one another. By this all people will know that you are my disciples, if you have love* (agape) *for one another.* (John 13:34-35)

The old commandment was to love one another as yourself. It's called the Golden Rule. The new commandment is radically different. Maybe we should call it the Diamond Rule. Currently, a choice diamond is worth more than 200% of the same amount of gold. That is a good comparison of agape love to the Golden Rule kind of love. The new commandment means that you care more for the other person than you do for yourself. That's agape love. It is through loving others selflessly that we are identified as Jesus' people. Because agape love is who Jesus is, agape love is to be who we are becoming. That's the love Jesus gave and continues to give to his people. Agape love always costs the giver. Agape love is in every believer.

Under the inspiration of the Holy Spirit, Paul wrote to the church in Rome explaining to them that *God's love has been poured into our hearts through the Holy Spirit who has been given to us.* (Romans 5:5) Followers of Jesus have agape love within them because we have the Spirit present in us. Notice these descriptive liquid analogies. God's love is *poured* into our hearts. Because we already have that love within, we ask that our agape love will *fill up* and *overflow* out of us so that it splashes onto everyone around us.

Our greatest need is for agape love to super-abound in us with increasing measure. Isn't this true in your life? May I answer that for you? Yes, it's true for you because it's true for every believer walking on planet earth. If you're a husband or a parent, you know the need to have your agape love continually increasing. Fellow husbands, we are commanded by God to agape love our wives all the time, 24/7, 7 days/week, 52 weeks/year. It's not an option. This is our calling. (Ephesians 5:22-33) In 35 years of marriage, I have found it extremely easy to agape love my wife and to always put her wants and needs well above my own. It's a piece of cake - that I just choked on. Of course it's incredibly difficult to agape love your wife all the time. The Me Monster within us is constantly vying for first place. What do you need? If you're already agape loving her with the Spirit's help, you need to ask the Father to make your agape love increase and abound more and more. If you're not doing too well in the agape love category, then maybe you should ask your heavenly Father to grant you to be strengthened with power through his Spirit so that the Lord Jesus can dwell in your heart through faith, making you rooted and grounded in agape love. (Kingdom Come Prayer #2, Chapter 4)

Paul cheered the Philippian church to even further acts of agape love: *Therefore if you have any encouragement from being united with Christ, if any comfort from his love* (agape), *if any common sharing in the Spirit, if any tenderness and compassion, then make my joy complete by being like-minded, having the same love* (agape), *being one in spirit and of one mind. Do nothing out of selfish ambition or vain conceit. Rather, in humility value others above yourselves, not looking to your own interests but each of you to the interests of the others. In your relationships with one another, have the same mindset as Christ Jesus:* (2:1-5, NIV)

The Spirit defined agape love by stating that it is putting the interests of others above your own. Agape love is humbling yourself and caring more about the other person than you do about yourself. Please don't try this without Jesus. You'll hurt yourself!

You can never have too much agape love. What drives this request for the Kingdom to come about in the heart of a believer is the realization that agape love is present, but lacking. Because you are giving agape love out to others, you're going to need your agape love tank replenished. Because your agape love sometimes leaks or even evaporates in stressful times, you're going to need to ask God to give you more and more of his powerful love.

This request for an increasing flow of agape love is multi-directional; it's up and out. God no doubt wants us to agape love him more and more – no conditions. If life is good, we are lovingly devoted and when life is tough and times are hard, we still love him with our whole being. God longs for our love for the Father, the Son and the Holy Spirit to continue in unwavering devotion.

His will is for our agape love to overflow towards him in constant praise and thanksgiving. How often do you thank God for what he has done and is doing in and through you? Me too. I don't thank him like he deserves. What's the remedy? Ask him to make your agape love increase and abound upward, for him.

His will is also that your agape love will continue to grow outward, to the people that he loves so dearly and who he has placed in your circle of influence. It makes perfect Kingdom sense for agape love to be the most prominent in the homes of his people, within our most intimate relationships. If you can't give agape love to your spouse and children, how can your public acts of kindness and generosity truly be genuine agape love? Imagine how God is glorified and pleased when agape love pours out from his local churches into the schools, the neighborhoods and the places of business where his people live, work and study.

Agape love is a Who

Agape love isn't really a characteristic of the maturing believe, it is who they are and who they are becoming. The maturing follower of Jesus is an apprentice of the Lord Jesus and is not just learning his trade, they are becoming the same kind of person as their Master. God is love and he is in us. Agape love is to define who we are, not necessarily what we do. Jesus' picture of this is vivid in his story about how it will all go down when he returns. If you enjoy reading about the end times, one of the best places to study is in Matthew 24-25. Jesus concluded his teaching about the end times with a graphic story. The bottom line in this story is this: his followers served the poor, the destitute and prisoners out of their agape love. They didn't do good deeds to earn a reward. Their good deeds flowed out of the abundance of agape love in their hearts, the agape love that God was increasing day by day. The "righteous" people served others, not for what they could get out of it, but because of what God had poured into them. Their good deeds were the supernatural result of agape love overflowing from them more and more and splashing out on those they came in contact with through the course of their normal day. Read Matthew 25:31-46. I find it a great gut-check motivator that reminds me of what really matters in life.

Full knowledge and complete discretion

Let's take another look at the request: *And it is my prayer that your love may abound more and more, with knowledge and all discernment.* Agape love doesn't abound more and more in gushy, hand-holding, Kumbaya love fests. Agape love grows with full knowledge and keen discernment. The word for knowledge is the same word used in the first Kingdom Come Prayer from Ephesians 1:17-19. So the unique thing about agape love is that it abounds more and more in razor-sharp understanding and keen discretion. Wise insights to know what to do, what to say and when to say it come from the agape love that is overflowing more and more from you.

You've experienced that tension of not knowing what to say or when to say it. Often the timing is more important than the words spoken. How do you avoid those relational pot holes? Ask God to make your agape love grow in insight and discernment so that you will know just how to respond and when to remain silent.

Can we take a quick trip down a short rabbit trail about when to be silent? When people get upset, their brain changes. The brain doesn't work like it normally does. When people get angry, the neo cortex portion of the brain goes on vacation. That's the part of the brain that gives us reason and rationale. When upset, the limbic system kicks in, which is all a rat brain has. That's why rats either fight or flea as a defense mechanism. That means when you get angry, you aren't the same rational thinking, agape loving person you normally are. There's more bad news. You actually lose IQ points, as many as 20-30! If you are an average 100 on the IQ scale, then you could slip down into the "Borderline Mentally Impaired" category when you get angry. The good news is that you get those points back once you calm down. This explains a lot doesn't it? That's why you've said things and done things that you would otherwise never have said or done. The acronym WAIT is helpful: Why Am I Talking? Agape love's insights and discernment will help you to keep your mouth shut when you're upset. It will empower you to wait until you calm down before you reply to that text or on Facebook.

The famous love passage

We're told exactly what agape love is in 1 Corinthians 13:1-8a. This passage is frequently used at wedding ceremonies, which is fine, but the context of the passage has to do with relationships within the church. In Chapters 12-14, Paul explained and illustrated that every church is stronger through the diversity of the people who make up the church and what each one contributes. He explained that the most important characteristic of every believer is not their talents or spiritual abilities, it is their agape love.

If I speak human or angelic languages
but do not have love,
I am a sounding gong or a clanging cymbal.

If I have the gift of prophecy
and understand all mysteries
and all knowledge,
and if I have all faith
so that I can move mountains
but do not have love, I am nothing.
And if I donate all my goods to feed the poor,
and if I give my body in order to boast
but do not have love, I gain nothing.
Love is patient, love is kind.
Love does not envy,
is not boastful, is not conceited,
does not act improperly,
is not selfish, is not provoked,
and does not keep a record of wrongs.
Love finds no joy in unrighteousness
but rejoices in the truth.
It bears all things, believes all things,
hopes all things, endures all things.
Love never ends. (1 Corinthians 13:1-8a, HCSB)

Did you notice how love is personified in this passage? That's because love *is* a person; God is love. He doesn't have love; he is love. Because the Spirit of God inhabits us, agape love is ours. It only needs to grow and keep on growing.

Agape love grows in complete knowledge and depth of insight. Full knowledge and deep discernment guides us as to how we should express agape love in any and every situation we face. Agape love wisely guides us to be able to do what's right no matter how difficult the decision. Notice that agape love abounds more and more *with* knowledge and all discernment. They are inseparable. Agape love produces complete knowledge and deep perception. We're commanded to speak the truth in agape love and that will help us to grow up in every way into Christ. (Ephesians 4:15) Agape love grows with an increasing discernment of how to speak the truth, what to say, what not to say, and when to say it. Agape love brings with it the ability to distinguish between rational lies and the truth. It gives the knowledge of what is black, white and grey. Agape love sets us free from being self-focused by giving us the wisdom to take up our own cross and die to self-centered choices and desires. Got agape? Is it increasing? Then ask for it every day. Praying for agape love to overflow more and more has tremendous results.

Result #1 – Determining what's excellent

Life is full of decisions. Do I buy my teen the cell phone they want? Do I replace the car now? Should I invest in a CD or Money Market account? Should I go for that promotion? Should we go out for dinner? How much should I give to the missions project at church? Life is full of big decisions and little decisions and every size in between. God wants you to ask that your agape love will overflow more and more *so that you may approve what is excellent and so be pure and blameless on the day of Christ.* (1:10) The word translated "approve" can also be translated discern, recognize, determine, choose or see. God wants you to be able to recognize the excellent choice. He wants you, through agape love, to see the superior option. The word translated "excellence" can also be translated best, superior and important. Therefore, what happens to us as our agape love increases with knowledge and all discernment is that we grow in our ability to recognize what is the excellent thing to do and to say. We'll know what the best solution is, based on agape love increasing within us.

Excellence isn't perfection. Excellence is giving our absolute best within the context of our current resources. Excellence honors God and inspires people. You've been part of a worship service that you would describe as excellent. It wasn't flawless, but you had the sense that God was honored and those in attendance were inspired. You've experienced excellence at work or school. Wasn't it inspiring? Didn't it make you want to give your best? A personal core value of excellence will help you to avoid the plague of mediocrity. We owe God our very best in everything we do. That's why the Bible commands us: *And whatever you do, in word or deed, do everything in the name of the Lord Jesus, giving thanks to God the Father through him.* (Colossians 3:17) Doing and saying excellent things in the name of the Lord Jesus means that we're conscious of his presence, so we want to please him because he's watching and listening. Doing everything in the name of Jesus demands our best, given the time and energy we have for that specific task. Giving our best comes from a growing agape love within.

A truth like this can be twisted by a student who justifies that they studied as hard as they could with the time they had. When in fact, they spent most of the evening before the test playing video games or texting with friends. It can look the same at work. Maybe you don't like a certain part of your job responsibilities so you spend more time on the things you like to do and give those other tasks a passing glance. That kind of attitude is far from doing everything in the name of the Lord Jesus. Giving your best means you give it all you have, regardless of who sees it or doesn't. In Ephesians 6:5-8, we are instructed to give our best at work, or at school, and to do it as if Jesus himself is our boss or teacher. So increasing your agape love can have a profound impact on how you perform on the job or how you do your school work. Do you need a little pick-me-up in that arena? Ask the Father to increase your agape love.

Thinking excellent thoughts is what Paul admonished the believers in Philippi to do: *Finally, brothers, whatever is true, whatever is honorable, whatever is just, whatever is pure, whatever is lovely, whatever is commendable, if there is any excellence, if there is anything worthy of praise, think about these things.* (Philippians 4:8) What is the best thing for you to be thinking about? It's beautifully described in this verse. How in the world can you control your thoughts so they linger on this list? Ask the Father to make your agape love abound more and more with full knowledge and all discernment so you can see what is excellent to think about.

With God's gracious help, you can have a mind in which the Lord Jesus is so present that he gradually crowds out your old way of thinking. Imagine the Lord Jesus never being more than a deliberate thought away! All you have to do is to take control of your thinking and allow the reality of the Spirit's presence to have his proper influence. How can you take control of your thinking? Ask the Father to help you. Ask him to make your agape love increase in deep wisdom and rich insights so that you can recognize what is best and set your mind on what Jesus values instead of the things of this world. It's difficult but possible, with God's gracious help. And it's well worth every effort that you can give it.

Agape love produces excellence

Growing in agape love gives us the wisdom to

recognize what is the best thing to say or do. How many times have you been in a situation and you didn't know what to say? It's a regular reality in marriage and raising children. It probably happens to most of us every day at work or at school. We're not completely sure what to do, how to respond, or when to say what needs to be said. Too often we react like Sara Bareilles lyrics, "Say what you wanna say, and let the words fall out..." I would love to get a do-over for the countless times that unkind words fell out of my mouth without passing through the filter of agape love.

Increasing agape love allows us to be able to determine what is best in the heat of the battle. This prayer is my "go-to" flare prayer. When a harsh email arrives, an unkind word is spoken or I feel disrespected, my greatest need is to be able to respond through the powerful wisdom of agape love. Otherwise, I'll react from my old Me Monster self and it will not be pretty. Been there, done that, got the trophy! That's why praying a quick request for agape love to abound right now can lead to just the right wisdom and discernment to handle the situation in a Jesus-pleasing way.

The way to protect yourself from believing rational lies or going Rat Brain is to continually ask the Father to make your agape love overflow so that you can have crystal clear vision to recognize what is the best course of action to take. The love of Christ and the love for Christ come to us through the indwelling Spirit of Christ so that we can do what is excellent from Christ's perspective. Ask for it. That's how the Kingdom comes in you.

As an example, let's say your co-worker confides in you that they are in a full-blown affair and contemplating leaving their spouse to run off with their new lover.

You're completely caught off guard. What do you say? What questions can you ask to give them the right guidance? You know that God's will is one man, one woman, in a life-long covenant of marital fidelity. But how do you explain it? Ask God to make your agape love for your co-worker to overflow more and more so that you'll have the wisdom to know the best thing to say at just the right time. Your abounding agape love will take you to your knees to pray for your co-worker, asking God to flood their heart with the light of Christ so that they can see their sin and the hurt and chaos they are causing. You continue praying for them and each time you see them at work, you fire off a flare prayer asking for your agape love to overflow so that you will know the best way to respond in each conversation. You trust that God will give you the ability to determine when you need to confront them and how to encourage them to make the right choice. The excellent way is to keep praying for them and for yourself, that your agape love grows with knowledge and discernment so that you can see what God wants you to do and what he wants you to say.

It is excellent when we obey all that Jesus commanded. It is even more excellent when we stand, in agape love, with another believer to help them embrace obedience to the Lord. The idea that you shouldn't get involved or that you have no business telling someone what to do comes from the pit of hell and smells like smoke! If a car in front of you keeps drifting towards the center-line, aren't you going to do something to help them? You'll blow your horn or flash your lights or call 911; you'll do something. You can't just sit back and watch them wreck. If a fellow follower is drifting away from living for Jesus, agape love will drive you to take action. Increasing agape love will give you the discernment of what action to take and when to take it, but you must keep your life focused on the future, not only on today.

The day of Christ

The result of praying for a growing agape love isn't focused only on the here and now. The primary focus is on the day that Jesus returns to earth. Let's consider it further: *so that you may approve what is excellent and so be pure and blameless on the day of Christ.* The day of Christ is the Second Coming, when Jesus will appear visibly to end all evil, judge the world, give us new immortal bodies and create a new earth where we will live with him for an ageless age. Pretty good "day", huh?

Paul used the phrase two other times in this short letter. *I am sure of this, that he who began a good work in you will bring it to completion at the day of Jesus Christ.* (1:6) The excellent things their love and faith were driving them to do would be brought to full completion when Jesus returns. Paul encouraged them that they were lights in the world who were *holding fast to the word of life, so that in the day of Christ* (2:16) he would be proud that his ministry with them was not in vain. The New Testament churches kept the reality of the return of Jesus in the forefront of their thinking and living. A growing agape love for God will bring about a more focused eternal perspective.

We can develop a stronger focus on Jesus' return by asking the Father to make our agape love grow and keep growing. As our love for God grows, our minds are opened up further to recognize what is excellent and to have a desire to live blamelessly before him. The first result from this Kingdom Come Prayer produces the ability to see what is best so we will live pure and blameless lives because Jesus is coming back and his return is imminent. It could happen at any moment.

To live blamelessly means that we are growing in our love for the Lord. Jesus made it very clear that love for him always produces obedience to him. People who say they know Jesus but don't obey his commands are liars. Those are not my words, the apostle John wrote this truth in 1 John 2:4. If you don't have a compelling desire to obey all of Jesus' teachings and thus live blamelessly, ask the Father to grant you to be strengthened with power through his Spirit in your inner being, which is the second Kingdom Come Prayer. Living blamelessly also means that you are keeping short accounts with God and regularly confessing your sins and forgiving everyone who owes you something. Forgive as you have been forgiven.

One of two things is most definitely going to happen to you. Either you will leave here and meet him there, or he will come here and you will meet him in the air. Your life is racing towards a face to face meeting with Jesus the Christ, the Lamb of God, our Lord and Savior. The moment you die, you will be found immediately in his presence. If Jesus returns while you are still alive, you will witness his stunningly glorious return and you will be taken up to meet him in the sky. (1 Thessalonians 4:13-18) One of those is going to take place and you don't know the day or time of either one. Therefore, the most excellent thing you can do is to develop a more heavenly perspective that is fueled by agape love abounding more and more in and through you.

Just after writing this prayer, Paul shared with the church in Philippi of his dilemma in 1:19-26. His deep desire was to be with the Lord, which obviously meant he would have to die. He wasn't suicidal, he just knew how much better it would be to live in Jesus' visible presence. Paul had faced death several times because of his faith in Christ. He knew that living in the presence of Jesus in the next life far surpassed anything this life had to offer. He *really* knows that now! But he also wanted to continue his ministry here on earth, so he was torn, with one foot in this life and the other in the real life.

Don't you want to have more of an eternal focus? Wouldn't it be so much more fun to know exactly how to respond to people in any given situation? The opportunity for both of these is ours. "Dear Father, make my agape love overflow more and more in full knowledge and complete discernment so that I can determine what is best and be pure and blameless until Jesus returns." But wait! There's one more result from this kind of praying.

Result #2 – Filled with the fruit of righteousness

The second result of asking for agape love to increase and keep growing is to be: *filled with the fruit of righteousness that comes through Jesus Christ, to the glory and praise of God.* One of Jesus' favorite metaphors was fruit. The word is used 66 times in 56 verses in the New Testament. All but 13 of those verses are in the Gospels. His audience was dependent on the crops and fruit that were harvested. From fig trees to grape vines and wheat, the edible part of the plant was its fruit. So in Jesus day, fruit was critically important to sustaining life. That's why Jesus frequently used the metaphor of their good deeds and right character as being good fruit. We need to understand what *the fruit of righteousness* means for us today.

Jesus gave his most graphic illustration of fruit

bearing the night he was arrested, in John 15:1-17. I find it helpful to think about the fact that the apostle John wrote his account of the life of Jesus when John was a very old man. He outlived all the other apostles and most likely wrote his letters some 30 years after all the other portions of the New Testament were written. The Spirit led John to give us Jesus' final teaching to his disciples that Thursday night before he was crucified. The teaching takes up Chapters 13-17 in John's Gospel. The wording indicates that Chapters 13-14 occurred in the Upper Room of the home they were using and Chapters 15-17 happened as they traveled the road to the Garden of Gethsemane. Try and picture our Lord walking along the road that night with his disciples, and when he comes to a lush vineyard beside the road, he stops and opens their minds to the Kingdom.

> "*I am the true vine, and My Father is the vineyard keeper. Every branch in Me that does not produce fruit He removes, and He prunes every branch that produces fruit so that it will produce more fruit. You are already clean because of the word I have spoken to you. Remain in Me, and I in you. Just as a branch is unable to produce fruit by itself unless it remains on the vine, so neither can you unless you remain in Me.*
>
> *I am the vine; you are the branches. The one who remains in Me and I in him produces much fruit, because you can do nothing without Me. If anyone does not remain in Me, he is thrown aside like a branch and he withers. They gather them, throw them into the fire, and they are burned. If you remain in Me and My words remain in you, ask whatever you want and it will be done for you. My Father is glorified by this: that you produce much fruit and prove to be My disciples.*
>
> *As the Father has loved Me, I have also loved you.*

> *Remain in My love. If you keep My commands you will remain in My love, just as I have kept My Father's commands and remain in His love.*
>
> *I have spoken these things to you so that My joy may be in you and your joy may be complete. This is My command: Love one another as I have loved you. No one has greater love than this, that someone would lay down his life for his friends. You are My friends if you do what I command you. I do not call you slaves anymore, because a slave doesn't know what his master is doing. I have called you friends, because I have made known to you everything I have heard from My Father. You did not choose Me, but I chose you. I appointed you that you should go out and produce fruit and that your fruit should remain, so that whatever you ask the Father in My name, He will give you. This is what I command you: Love one another."* (John 15:1-17, HCSB)

Jesus is the life-giving vine. His love and righteousness are like the water and nutrients that are passed from the vine to the branches. We are his branches and our purpose is to produce fruit, lots and lots of luscious, delicious fruit. If the vine is healthy, the branches will produce fruit, provided each one remains completely attached to the vine. The fruit of the Spirit is: *love, joy, peace, patience, kindness, goodness, faithfulness, gentleness and self-control.* (Galatians 5:22-23a) Now read Jesus teaching in John 15 one more time.

Notice the brilliant way that Jesus wove agape love into the illustration of producing fruit. Keeping Jesus' commands is how we love him and his command is that we agape love other believers. In this way, our lives will produce fruit that will last for all eternity. That fruit, my friends, is the impact and influence our lives have on other people. The impact is eternal because only the souls of boys and girls, teenagers and men and women will remain forever. Our fruit is about inspiring, encouraging, guiding, teaching, admonishing and influencing people. Jesus chose us to produce righteous fruit that remains "*so that whatever you ask the Father in My name, He will give you.*"

Will the Father answer your prayer about increasing your agape love? Of course he will. Jesus knows that as long as we stay connected to him and remain in his love, we will produce fruit and his Father will be honored. There's nothing Jesus wants to do more than to honor his Father.

Let's think again about the second result of asking for agape love to abound more and more: to be *filled with the fruit of righteousness that comes through Jesus Christ, to the glory and praise of God.* The impact of our right actions and words, what those produce, comes through Jesus Christ. That is what Jesus described in the vine and branch illustration. Agape love and every good deed that flows out of us only does so as it comes into us through Jesus. It's the reality of the vine and the branches. All that is good in you is because of Jesus being in you. Praise God for that!

Do you want more righteous fruit to be produced through your life? Do you want to have a greater impact on the people you do life with? Do you want to leave a holy legacy? Of course you do, especially if you're this far along in this book. Therefore, ask the Father to make your agape love overflow more and more in full knowledge of his Word and his ways and in complete discernment of the situation you're dealing with. Then you will be able to determine what is excellent, the best thing to do, and you'll be pure and blameless until Jesus returns, filled with right actions and attitudes that come through Jesus Christ. Your life will bring praise and glory to God. Ask him to do that and keep on asking every day and multiple times throughout the day. The results will be astounding.

The Philippians gave as much money as they could, by God's great grace, to the starving believers in Israel. *Now God who provides seed for the sower and bread for food will provide and multiply your supply of seed and will cause the harvest of your righteousness to grow. You will be enriched in every way so that you may be generous on every occasion, which is producing through us thanksgiving to God, because the service of this ministry is not only providing for the needs of the saints but is also overflowing with many thanks to God. Through the evidence of this service they will glorify God because of your obedience to your confession in the gospel of Christ and the generosity of your sharing with them and with everyone. And in their prayers on your behalf they long for you because of the extraordinary grace God has shown to you. Thanks be to God for his indescribable gift!* (2 Corinthians 9:10-15)

We have the opportunity, every day, to serve others so that they will thank God because of our growing agape love. As he increases our agape love, we will be able to do and say the kinds of things that will inspire others to thank God. If they want to praise you instead, you will have the opportunity to explain to them how it is the power of God's agape love working in and through you rather than your own goodness. Expressing your agape love to others in knowledge and all discernment will open up new opportunities to tell people about the hope you have in Christ Jesus.

May the grace of the Lord Jesus Christ be with your spirit. (Philippians 4:23)

Small Group Questions

1. Compare the request in this prayer (page 143) with the second Kingdom Come Prayer request in Ephesians 3:16 (page 98). How do you envision using them?

2. How do you understand the relationship between agape love, full knowledge and all discernment (page 148-149)? Think back to a time when you experienced the wisdom and insights of agape love.

3. Read the agape love passage from 1 Corinthians 13 on pages 149-150. Which of those aspects of agape love have you recently experienced from another follower of Christ?

4. Read the first result again on page 151. How does the promise of being able to recognize the best choice make you feel? How might this result influence your praying?

5. Read again John 15:1-17 (pages 159-160) and discuss your takeaways from Jesus' teaching. How can you grow in your agape love? What will you do?

Close your time together by praying through this prayer as a group

Kingdom Come Prayer #3

Philippians 1:9-11

THE REQUEST

Dear Father, make my agape love overflow more and more in full knowledge and complete discernment…

1st Result

so that I can determine what is excellent and be pure and blameless until the day of Christ…

2nd Result

so that I can be filled with the fruit of righteousness that comes through Jesus Christ, to your glory and praise.

Chapter 6 - Kingdom Come Prayer #4 Spiritual Wisdom & Power

For this reason also, since the day we heard this, we haven't stopped praying for you. We are asking that you may be filled with the knowledge of His will in all wisdom and spiritual understanding, so that you may walk worthy of the Lord, fully pleasing to Him, bearing fruit in every good work and growing in the knowledge of God. May you be strengthened with all power, according to His glorious might, for all endurance and patience, with joy giving thanks to the Father, who has enabled you to share in the saints' inheritance in the light. (Colossians 1:9-12, HCSB)

The fourth Kingdom Come Prayer parallels the prayers in Ephesians Chapters 1 and 3. In chapter 1, the request is to know God better and in Chapter 3 it is to be strengthened with his power. The prayer in Colossians 1 has two requests, one for knowledge and one for strengthening. Although the requests are similar, the results are different. Before we dig into the prayer itself, let's reflect back to how we use this kind of a prayer, according to Jesus' outline.

Jesus gave us the Followers' Prayer outline in Luke 11. To help you own it, it's summarized on page 55. He guided us through a 5 step outline that begins by acknowledging who God is and what he is like, then he taught us to ask for his kingdom to come. The "kingdom come" part of the prayer outline is asking our Father to bring about spiritual transformation in us and in the lives of the people we pray for. That transformation is what we have been studying the past three chapters, from the prayers in Ephesians and Philippians. As you become more and more comfortable with the Kingdom Come Prayers, you will discover when to use which request as well as how to combine requests. I have found it helpful to keep a summary sheet of the prayers in my Bible. A summary sheet of each prayer is provided on pages 91, 137, 165 and 209. A two-page, front and back summary of all four of the Kingdom Come Prayers is on pages 231-232. These pages can be torn out of the book so that you can keep it with you.

It is critically important to understand that when Jesus taught his disciples how to pray, he taught them to ask for spiritual formation first, and physical needs next. Beginning your prayers by focusing on the spiritual formation prayers in the Bible will impact the rest of your praying. Remember, Jesus taught us very plainly to begin by asking for the Kingdom to come. Next, we are to ask the Father to give us our *daily bread,* which encompasses all of the tangible things we need for life. He already knows everything that we need. Through asking him to provide for us each day, we will grow in our reliance on him, recognizing more and more that everything good in our life comes directly from the Father of Lights. After making these requests, we are in a perfect position, spiritually and emotionally, to confess our sins and then release everyone from every debt we might be holding over their heads. Lastly in the Followers' Prayer, we are to acknowledge that we live in God's continual presence, and we need him to show us the way out of every temptation and to protect us from all evil and the Evil One.

A Kingdom focus

Kingdom Come Praying, according to Jesus' model for us, is the first area of requests. It might be helpful to think about these prayers as preventative maintenance prayers. Much of our praying is fueled by some crisis or a challenging problem to overcome. What typically drives you to pray? In your small group or Bible study, how would you categorize the majority of the prayer requests? Very often our prayers are only about the daily bread sort of issues of health, safety and finances. Kingdom Come Praying can completely change your perspective about the crisis at hand. Like pit crews that constantly make adjustments to the car throughout the race, continual and "God's will" praying throughout each day is how we can remain in Christ, enjoying the hope and peace of knowing his presence. The goal is to develop a Kingdom Come mindset that drives you to ask your Father to increase your knowledge and strength to follow Jesus.

A little later in the letter, Paul gave us one of the most challenging passages in all of Scripture: *If then you have been raised with Christ, seek the things that are above, where Christ is, seated at the right hand of God. Set your minds on things that are above, not on things that are on earth. For you have died, and your life is hidden with Christ in God. When Christ who is your life appears, then you also will appear with him in glory.* (Colossians 3:1-4) It almost feels impossible to pull this off. How can you really stop focusing on the stuff of this life and set your desires on your life in Christ and the new world to come?

Did you notice how the Spirit led Paul to use two parallel statements? The *things above* are what we are to desire. The things that are above is also where we are to focus our thinking. This means our thinking and our emotions are both to be locked and loaded on Jesus, where he is right now, what he is doing, what he is going to do, what he is like and what heaven is like. The way to keep your mind and emotions Christ-centric is to incorporate the Kingdom Come Prayers into your normal conversations with your Father during the course of each day. Learning to pray this way throughout the day forces you to think about the Lord so that you can learn to desire more of what he desires. Asking the Father to fill you with the knowledge of his will and to strengthen you with his power *is* seeking the things above, where Christ is seated. These prayers set your mind and your emotions on Jesus, which will help to release the tight grip that the stuff of this life has on you.

It takes perseverance

When Paul wrote these words to the Colossians, he had never met them or visited their church. A member of his team, Epaphras, told him all about the church; maybe Epaphras couldn't stop talking about their practical faith and their selfless love for all the saints. They agape loved other believers whether they attended their church or not: *He (*Epaphras*) is a faithful minister of Christ on your behalf and has made known to us your love in the Spirit.* (Colossians 1:7b-8)

Paul wrote that since the very day they heard about

this great church, he and his team were in constant prayer for them. Constant prayer is our directive as the people of God. It must be a top priority for every pastor, elder, deacon, director, bishop and ministry leader in every church. But persistent praying is not the responsibility of just the pastors and leaders. All followers of Jesus are to regularly exercise our high privilege of praying in order to deepen our devotion to the Lord and to see his kingdom come about in every family in our church.

Paul makes this clear in his first letter to the church in the city of Thessalonica when he wrote this short command, *pray without ceasing.* (1 Thessalonians 5:17). The whole church was directed to pray all the time. This means that prayer is part of the on-going activity that we do every day. Imagine how your life can change as you build regular pray into your daily routine. Some prayers are short and some are more concentrated, but praying to our Father is to be continual. If praying is going to be a constant activity in your normal day, then most of those prayers are going to be short and to the point.

The Spirit inspired Paul to encourage the believers in the church in Colossae in a similar way. *Continue steadfastly in prayer, being watchful in it with thanksgiving.* (Colossians 4:2) Consider how other translations phrase this idea: *Continue earnestly in prayer* (NKJV) and *devote yourselves to prayer* (HCSB, NASB, NLT and NIV,). This is the same message to the Thessalonians. This is the message Jesus gave us as illustrated in the story of the midnight traveler and the persistent widow (pages 3-5). God wants us to continue in constant prayer, talking to him about all the things that concern us both.

Epaphras, Paul's faithful co-minister and a member of the Colossae Community Church, prayed regularly for his fellow saints. At the end of the letter, Paul shared: *Epaphras, who is one of you, a servant of Jesus Christ, greets you, struggling on your behalf in his prayers, that you may stand mature and fully assured in all the will of God.* (Colossians 4:12). Epaphras may be the poster child of persistent prayer, but he must not stand alone. God's calling on each of us is to struggle in prayer just like Epaphras did. It is a struggle. We should learn how to wrestle in prayer. Learning Jesus' outline of the Followers' Prayer, using it daily and learning these Kingdom Come Prayers is not easy. However, it is likely the most rewarding work you will ever do, because you will be praying according to God's will and the results are eternal. What drove Epaphras? He longed for all the members of his church to stand firm in their faith, mature and complete, confident that they were living in the will of God.

To pray diligently without stopping is sort of like texting. It doesn't mean that you never stop texting; it means you always have your phone with you so that you can send texts as needed, throughout the day. During each day, you have times when you need to pray, but you don't have the time to work through Jesus' outline. In those times, flare prayers are an effective way to live in the consciousness of God's presence, reminding yourself how much you, and those you are praying for, need the Lord's help. Flare prayers are also flare praises when you thank God for the beauty of the day or the way he just gave you his grace to respond, or not respond. I have found these two requests in the Colossians' prayer to be powerfully practical flare prayers. I have asked God to strengthen me with all power or fill me with the knowledge of his will in all wisdom and spiritual understanding countless times, often in the heat of the moment. The times I have flared one of these prayers for my wife, Tammy, or our children, or their spouses are too numerous to write about. I have experienced our Father giving his wisdom and power to me and to those I prayed for countless times. He does what we ask of him. God answers our requests as we pray for the things he wants to give us. You can be assured of that reality. This prayer in Colossians Chapter 1 is precisely what he wants to give to all of his dearly loved people who ask him. Let's consider the first request.

REQUEST #1 - Filled with knowledge

We are asking that you may be filled with the knowledge of His will in all wisdom and spiritual understanding. (Colossians 1:9-12, HCSB) God wants you to know his will for your life. He not only wants you to know it, he wants the *full* knowledge of his will to *fill* your mind and your soul. He wants you to want to know his will for you life, in the big decisions and the daily ones, too. But you need his help to have confidence that you can understand his will. You need his help to have the desire to *want* to know his will. Being filled with the knowledge of his will is what happens when you set your heart and mind on the things above. The closer we get to God, the more intimately we know him. The more we understand his will, the more we will realize our constant dependence on him. We grow in our spirit through the help of his Spirit. God's will is to give you more of his Spirit's influence within your spirit to grow your wisdom and your understanding of his Word and his ways.

Doesn't it make sense that our Father in the heavens wants us to know his will for our lives? Is he the kind of Father who enjoys keeping us in the dark about his plans? Of course not! Since he is love, can he do anything other than communicate his desires to us as we ask him? No. Our loving, heavenly Father wants nothing more than to lead his children to have unwavering love and devotion for him. Let's dig in further.

The knowledge of his will

The request is *that you may be filled with the knowledge of his will in all wisdom and spiritual understanding.* (Colossians 1:9, HCSB) As we have discovered from the other Kingdom Come Prayers, the request is for a special kind of knowledge, a full and complete understanding of God and what he wants to happen. Paul was led to use this same Greek compound that he used repeatedly in the other Kingdom Come Prayers. This word depicts a full and complete knowledge. The request goes even further, asking for complete knowledge of God's will in the given circumstance or situation that we are facing.

What answers are you searching for right now? What is a current challenge that you are facing? What are the issues that those you love are wrestling with? Are you wondering what in the world God's will is for you in some area of your life? We all face that question. Life takes unexpected twists, tragedies happen, hopes are dashed and we wonder why God didn't intervene like we expected. Knowing God's will for us can be very confusing, if we make it confusing. God doesn't want you be confused or anxious about his will for your life. He wants you to trust him as you seek his direction and his leading.

Have there been times when you never considered asking God to show you his will? Haven't you caused personal fender benders in life because you didn't ask, seek or knock regarding what God wanted you to do? Haven't we all created unnecessary problems because we rushed in without asking God to guide us? It's easy to set a goal or pursue some desire and never consider how God might fit in to the equation because "I'll do it myself" is our human nature. At our core, we tend to think, "I've got this." What we think we can do on our own ranges widely, from our to-do list for the day to a career decision to marrying a spouse or having children. Our default as humans is to figure it out on our own or to ask others until someone finally tells us what we want to hear. Then a crisis hits and you realize you don't have it all figured out. Your plan wasn't the best way to go. This Kingdom Come Prayer request to know God's will can protect you from making plans and doing things without considering God's perspective. Imagine how much better life can be when you keep the desire to know God's will in the forefront of your thinking and planning? Wanting God's will more than your own plans is what being a disciple of Jesus Christ is all about. That is a huge part of denying yourself daily, taking up your own cross and following after Jesus. (Luke 9:23) Following Jesus leads us toward becoming the kind of people who want to keep in perfect harmony with the melody that our Father has written for us.

This is precisely how Jesus prayed in the Garden of Gethsemane on that Holy Thursday night. The suffering he was about to endure was completely overwhelming to him. The anguish was so great that Jesus' facial capillaries burst *and his sweat became like great drops of blood falling down to the ground.* (Luke 22:44) He repeatedly begged his Father for some other way: *And going a little farther he fell on his face and prayed, saying, "My Father, if it be possible, let this cup pass from me; nevertheless, not as I will, but as you will."* (Matthew 26:39) Don't ever think that Jesus only said this out of his deep respect for his Father.

Jesus was desperate. He begged his Abba Father. Jesus

did not want to suffer and die on the cross. The word excruciating means "out of the cross". We can not begin to fathom the spiritual suffering that Jesus endured on our behalf. The physical suffering was excruciating, but the spiritual suffering was so brutal that Isaiah described it this way: *Just as many were appalled at You, His appearance was so disfigured, that He did not look like a man, and His form did not resemble a human being* (Isaiah 52:14, HCSB) Because he knew the intensity of his coming suffering, Jesus pleaded with his Father to come up with some other way to redeem his people. He did not know any other way, because there wasn't one, yet he begged his Father three times to take this cup of suffering from him. He was in such emotional and spiritual distress that his Father sent an angel to strengthen him. (Luke 22:43) And yet, because Jesus was completely devoted to his Father, his greatest desire was to be obedient. More than anything, he was going to obey his Father. That is why he prayed for his Father's will to happen instead of his own desires. In the midst of his tears and fears, Jesus wanted to do exactly as his Father had planned. He is our Lord and Savior, and he is our model of how to surrender our will to follow God.

Surrendering your will for his

Your Father in the heavens wants you to become like his Son in his love and devotion. He wants to give you all the guidance, wisdom, insight and strength you need to be the person he desires. He wants you to ask him for his help by showing you the full knowledge of his will in every area of your life. Like his Son, he wants you to grow into the kind of person who wants his will to be the deciding factor, every time.

Knowing God's will is often presented as a bit of a

mystery. How can you be certain that you know God's will for your life? His general will for each of his sons and daughters is presented in this short letter to the believers in Colossae. His desire is for every believer to become mature in Christ (1:28), to live rooted in him, built up and established in the faith (2:7, 4:12) and to seek his kingdom above all else (3:1-4). There are many other ways that living according to the will of God is explicitly expressed in his Word. This letter to the Colossians contains almost all of the actions and attitudes a person will ever need to know to be able to understand God's will for how they should live. If we could just live out Colossians Chapter 3, we would be well on our way to living a life that fully pleases God.

Should you lie? Should you have sex outside of marriage? Should you forgive everyone who has offended you? Should you agape love those who don't love you back? Those are all easy answers that are clearly spelled out in this short chapter. God has given us his will for how we are to live in the Bible. It is not a mystery. It is written down for us in easy to understand chapters and verses.

However, we have lots of choices in life that are not spelled out so clearly. Should I pursue a promotion? Which courses should I take this semester? Should I date Hannah or Mandy, or both? Should I replace my car? How much should I give to my church or to that family in need? Should I home-school? What should I do about serving in my church? The daily questions we face can be overwhelming. The natural default to many of these questions is to try and figure it out on our own. Does God want to be involved in these decisions too? Of course he does. He is your Father in the heavens. He paid the ultimate price to purchase you from the domain of darkness. If you are the parent of adult children, doesn't it make you feel valued when your child asks you for your opinion?

Spiritual wisdom and understanding

The request is for God to fill you with the full knowledge of his will *in all wisdom and spiritual understanding*. The Greek literally reads: "in all wisdom and understanding spiritual". "Spiritual" modifies both wisdom and understanding. Then why isn't the word "spiritual" capitalized? Most English translators chose not to capitalize it because the context of the sentence conveys that God is giving us wisdom and understanding in our spirits. It is our spiritual wisdom and understanding that is growing. There is no doubt that our wisdom and our understanding are increasing through the influence of his Spirit. Because he lives in us, it is the Spirit of God who is giving us knowledge and insights, inspiring our spirits about the Father's will for us.

Who knows what's going to happen next year? Next week? Tomorrow? In the next two minutes? God does. As we learned in Chapter 3 of this book, the Spirit of God has all the knowledge and the know-how that you will ever need. He knows everything about everything! Therefore, knowing God's will comes through the understanding and wisdom that the Spirit gives us, in our spirit. It's the Spirit who gives you insights about how to apply God's truth to your situation when there isn't a specific go-to chapter and verse. The Spirit also brings to mind verses, passages or stories from the Bible that guide us into understanding the will of God. Doesn't the Spirit of Jesus frequently remind you of the teachings of Jesus? Nod "yes" with me.

What if the specific answer isn't as important as the process? Let's say you are facing a situation at work or school, and you don't know what to do. As you ask God, and keep asking him, to fill you with the knowledge of his will in all spiritual wisdom and understanding about what to do, you are already understanding his will. In the process of asking you are learning how to rely on God, which is his will for you. By reorienting your desire to want to know how to respond in a way that pleases God, you are living in the center of his will for your life. Even if in the end, you're not sure if you got it exactly right, as long as you sought the Lord's will through the process, you brought him great pleasure. Discerning God's answer about what is best to do or say is not always the end game. Learning to rely on him to help you understand his will is often the most important part of determining the will of God.

Remember how Jesus ended the story that followed him giving the disciples the prayer outline? He concluded this very intimate time of teaching about prayer with this truth: *"If you then, who are evil, know how to give good gifts to your children, how much more will the heavenly Father give the Holy Spirit to those who ask him?"* (Luke 11:13) The only way to know the will of the Father is when his Spirit communicates it to our hearts and minds. Often the way he does that is through our own Bible reading or by bringing certain verses to memory. There are obviously other ways as well. But the most important aspect of wanting the kingdom to come in our lives is to ask God to fill us with the knowledge of his will in all spiritual understanding and all spiritual wisdom, and to keep on asking. He will do just as Jesus said and give us his Spirit to come along beside us to direct our steps.

Filled 'er up

Lastly, the prayer request is to be *filled* with the knowledge of God's will. If you are filled up with understanding of his will, then there is no room in your heart and head for your own will, or her will or their will. How often have you felt compelled to carry out someone else's plans for your life? It sometimes feels like others are telling you: "God loves you, and *I* have a wonderful plan for your life." Being filled with God's will protects us from our own plans taking center stage and from being a puppet for someone else.

Being filled with God's will means that our sin tendencies are being crowded out. If a leadership team is filled with the knowledge of God's will, there will be unity and confidence in their decisions. A church that is seeking a new pastor, or considering a building program, needs to be filled with the knowledge of God's will to prevent divisions and to ensure that they are discerning together God's plans for them. The family that is filled with the knowledge of God's will may have tensions and many uncertainties about the decision they are making, but there will be unity and a sense of peace.

Have you noticed how easy it is to fill your mind and heart with all sorts of earthly things? Are you spending most of your mental energy thinking about future plans or challenges that you are currently facing? Concerns about your children, aging parents, finances, investments, insurance and retirement can easily steal your joy and consume your thinking. Our propensity is to be filled up with the cares of this life. The busier our lives become and the more stuff we own, the more prone we are to having our time and attention focused on *things that are on earth.* We must work diligently at keeping our hearts and heads filled with the things that really matter, the eternal destiny of the souls of boys and girls, teenagers and men and women. You can do it with God's help.

Flip back to page 153 and read Philippians 4:8 again. The Spirit said that we are to fill our minds with the things that fill his mind. How can you jettison your stinkin' thinkin' to be filled with God's way of thinking? Ask him. Keep crying out to your Father in the heavens, the One who arranged the stars and knows your every thought, to fill you with the complete knowledge of his will in the wisdom and insights that come from his Spirit into your spirit. Ask and don't stop asking, and your Father will fill you with his Holy Spirit. Does being filled with the Spirit mean you will do lots of whacky things? No, it means you will want to obey all that Jesus taught, so that your life aligns with his life. To be filled with the Spirit means that he is the driving influence in your thoughts, words, texts, emails, actions and reactions. Let's look at the results you can expect to experience as you learn to ask and keep on asking for God to fill you with his wisdom, the very thing he wants to do.

Result #1 - So that you walk worthy

The first outcome of being filled with the full knowledge of God's will is: *so that you may walk worthy of the Lord, fully pleasing to Him.* (1:10a) In Jesus' day, to "walk" was a popular figure of speech to describe how people lived and conducted their lives. That is how it is used in this verse. You can replace "walk" with "live", if it makes more sense to you. Since the primary form of transportation in Jesus' day was walking, it's a perfect metaphor that dates back thousands of years, spanning the Old Testament period. Psalm 1, which King David likely wrote, begins:

Blessed is the man
who walks not in the counsel of the wicked,
nor stands in the way of sinners,
nor sits in the seat of scoffers;

David pictured a blessed man as one who did not walk with evil people who were opposed to the values of Yahweh. A thousand years later, Paul admonished the church in Ephesus: *I therefore, a prisoner for the Lord, urge you to walk in a manner worthy of the calling to which you have been called, with all humility and gentleness, with patience, bearing with one another in love, eager to maintain the unity of the Spirit in the bond of peace.* (Ephesians 4:1-3) Walking worthy of the Lord means that we are living in such a way that honors and acknowledges Jesus. To live *worthy of the calling to which we have been called* is a powerful reminder that we have been transformed and are constantly being renewed by God's goodness and grace. Our lives are to show it. The way we act and the things we say are being influenced by the infilling of the Holy Spirit.

The truth is that none of us are worthy of being God's people. We don't deserve his grace and forgiveness, not for a second. That's why it is called "grace". God gives us what we don't deserve because Jesus took upon himself what we did deserve, God's judgment for our sin-crimes. God's grace is working in you every day to help you to think, say and do what you would never have done on your own. He is constantly infusing your life with his Spirit's strength and wise influence. That is grace to live by. The most reasonable thing we can do is to ask God to fill us full with the understanding of what his will is, so that we can fully participate in his grace, living worthy of his calling.

For every attitude and action, you can evaluate your

worthiness with this question: Is this proper for someone who has been rescued and adopted by the Almighty? Imagine what your life can become as you keep this question in the forefront of your brain, repeating it throughout the day. God wants to help you and me make life-choices that are worthy of Kingdom People. Aren't you thankful that God isn't sitting on his throne, with arms folded, scowling down at us, just waiting for us to make a mistake? Instead, he is actively involved in our daily lives to renew our thinking and transform our behavior. He is leaning into us! Our Father fully expects that we too, because we have been given so much, will also be actively involved in this renewal process. Our gratitude for all he has done, is doing, and is going to do, will compel us to want to live worthy of our calling. Praying these Kingdom Come Prayers is precisely how you can fully participate in all he is doing in and through you, which gives our Father great pleasure.

A new life-script

To be filled with the understanding of God's will is his script for our lives. When we come to believe in Jesus as who he really is, we are given an entirely new script to follow. The plot is radically different and there is a brand new list of characters. The old script cast you as the star. But you were never intended to play the leading role! You were never created to be worshipped! (And neither were your children, so don't raise them as if you worship them because they cannot handle that pressure.) Jesus was always meant to play the leading role in everyone's script. Our challenge, because we are sinful by nature, is that we have the propensity to pick up the old script. Asking God to fill us with the full knowledge of his will is how we return to the Kingdom Script to get our lives back on track in his story. Not only is Jesus the leading character in the new script, your role is to be more concerned about all the other characters than you are about yourself. That's what agape love is all about. You are called to put others ahead of yourself. Jesus gave us a vivid word picture for what it means to live in God's script where Jesus is the star and we strive to help all the other characters: "*If anyone would come after me, let him deny himself and take up his cross daily and follow me. For whoever would save his life will lose it, but whoever loses his life for my sake will save it.*" (Luke 9:23-24)

You can make the Lord smile

To live worthy of the Lord means that your choices are bringing him pleasure. Isn't it interesting that the Spirit added this phrase to the outcome? Thinking about how our thoughts, words and actions impact Jesus is a helpful way to stay in step with the Holy Spirit. Alongside the question of whether this is proper as a follower of Jesus, is an equally important question: Does this please God? Caring about whether your decisions and reactions really do please God puts you in the center of his will. You may be frustrated that even though you *want* to please God, you keep falling into the same trap that you know is displeasing to your Father. God is more concerned about direction than perfection. For example, King David did a lot of terrible things. But we know him as "the man after God's own heart." How can someone, who committed adultery and then had her husband killed to try and hide the pregnancy, be worthy of such a title? David was broken when God made him aware of his sin. David was a man who was quick to repent. When he realized that he had sinned horribly against God, it cut him to the core: *Against you, you only, have I sinned and done what is evil in your sight.* (Psalm 51:4a) He was repentant and broken. It was a repentant heart rather than a stellar record of obedience that led others to call David "the man after God's own heart".

Jesus' parable of the prodigal son isn't about the son. (Luke 15:11-32) The story is about the gracious and loving father who forgave his sinful, now repentant, son. He not only forgave him, he lavished him with love and gifts as if his son had never humiliated the family. The father's smile beamed because his repentant son was now home. *He was lost, and is found.* (v32b)

How can you make God smile? Confess your sins regularly and turn from them. Ask him to fill you with full understanding of what he wants you to know and do. Ask him to give you recall of his Scriptures and to help you honor his commands by rightly applying them. Seek to understand his words and his ways by giving yourself to regular instruction and solid teaching. Be a participant in a local church and not an attender. Read the Bible daily and strive to absorb the truths you have been so graciously given. Ask your pastor or a trusted believer to help you understand what God is saying in his Word so that you will have full knowledge of his will. The Spirit has a plethora of resources available for you to grow in your understanding of God so that you can live worthy of his name and fully please him with all your choices. Ask and it will be given; seek and you will find; knock and the door will be opened wide for you. And don't worry about what you don't yet understand in the Bible. The Father only holds us responsible to live according to what we know today.

Or you can make the Spirit sad

The opposite of making the Father smile is grieving him. When the Jews rebelled against God by acting unfaithful to him, God was grieved (Psalm 78:40, Isaiah 63:10). Paul warned us: *And do not grieve the Holy Spirit of God, by whom you were sealed for the day of redemption.* (Ephesians 4:30) How do we grieve him? The next verse tells us. *Let all bitterness and wrath and anger and clamor and slander be put away from you, along with all malice.* We bring the Spirit sorrow when we return to living like our old self, listening to the Me Monster. You likely won't ever wake up in the morning with the thought, "I think I'll try to grieve the Spirit of Jesus today – to see if I can make him really sad." It's not intentional. However, we can get mentally lazy and forget to keep God in the center of our plans and our daily activities. We get busy and forget to think about him and the things above. Asking him to fill you with insights about his perfect will guards you from sliding down the slippery slope that leads to making the Holy Spirit sad.

Ask yourself regularly if the decision you are about to act on is pleasing to your Lord. Some find it helpful to try and picture Jesus standing alongside them in the decision, sensing his expression. Each time you sense that you are not living in a way that is honoring or pleasing to the Lord and not worthy of someone who has been lavished with grace, stop, drop and pray. Colossians 1:9 is a fantastic flare prayer that you can launch heavenward in a moments notice. "Father, give me understanding of your will right now, so I can honor you!" It may also be helpful to picture your bad attitude or actions being poured out of you like nasty water from old flowers. Picture God filling you with the crystal clear water of his wisdom and insights. Making choices that are worthy of God by doing what pleases him sets you up for the second outcome of the request to be filled with the knowledge of his will.

Result #2 - So that you bear fruit

As you ask your Father to fill you and those you pray for with the full knowledge of his will, *bearing fruit in every good work* (1:10b) will result. We explored the metaphor of fruit-bearing in the second result of KCP #3 (pages 158-162). The wording in this verse is a bit different, so let's unpack it. Notice that the phrase coveys the idea of good works. Similar to the metaphor "to walk", "to work" is another word picture that is widely used in the Scriptures. Both metaphors are used in a powerful verse that should probably be memorized by all of Jesus' followers: *For we are his workmanship, created in Christ Jesus for good works, which God prepared beforehand, that we should walk in them.* (Ephesians 2:10)

A good work is a good deed. Good deeds are not limited to actions but include words and thoughts. We are God's very workmanship, like a piece of art he is crafting, that has been created in Christ Jesus. One of the purposes for which we have been created in Christ is to do good works, which are righteous actions, attitudes and words. The amazing thing is that our good deeds aren't just random acts of kindness. They were planned by God before we were ever born. This truth tells us that God is very intentional about what he wants us to do and say. That's why the phrase, "God has a plan for your life", has been so popular. It is true. God saved you from the dominion of darkness so that you will do wonderful things for him and for others that will have an eternal impact. He has placed you in the family, neighborhood, school, vocation, of his choosing so that he can work in and through you to touch the lives of all with whom you have influence.

When you don't feel like you are doing much for the Kingdom, the solution is found in this prayer request. If you feel like what you are doing isn't bearing much fruit, the solution is to ask the Father to fill you up with the knowledge of his complete will. Trust that his Spirit will give your spirit all the wisdom and understanding needed to better apply God's script to what you are doing. The key is to continually ask, because that is how you will learn to live in his presence moment by moment.

Stop comparing fruit

Jesus told a captivating story about producing fruit. *And he told this parable: "A man had a fig tree planted in his vineyard, and he came seeking fruit on it and found none. And he said to the vinedresser, 'Look, for three years now I have come seeking fruit on this fig tree, and I find none. Cut it down. Why should it use up the ground?' And he answered him, 'Sir, let it alone this year also, until I dig around it and put on manure. Then if it should bear fruit next year, well and good; but if not, you can cut it down.'"* (Luke 13:6-9)

You are adored by the God of second chances, third chances, tenth chances and on and on. God is digging around your trunk and adding manure to help you grow. Maybe this book is kind of like manure. I hope you don't think it stinks! Your pastor, books you read and songs you sing are all like that manure that is helping you to grow in order that your life can yield the fruit you were saved to produce. God wants to give you his Spirit to help you produce all the fruit that he chose for you, before he ever created the world. Isn't that a mind-boggling thought? The wonderful thing about fruit production is that it is completely unique to each person, each family, each church, each ministry, each organization and each business. We can end the fruit comparing game once and for all.

Jesus sets us free from playing the comparison game. Our natural tendency is to look at each other's fruit and judge who is doing the best. Too often we get caught up in destructive conversations about a piece of *apparently* rotting fruit on someone else's tree. We have those kinds of conversations to help us feel more justified about the condition of our own crop. The reason that happens so much is that too many followers of Jesus are not confident in their own fruit production. To help all of us, those with lots of fruit and those who are short a few bushels, Jesus told a story about seeds falling in different kinds of soil in Matthew 13:1-9. A little later in vs18-23, he interpreted the parable. His general point was that many people hear God's truth but it doesn't "take root". They are like bad soil. For those who do hear and heed it, they are the good soil in the story. "*As for what was sown on good soil, this is the one who hears the word and understands it. He indeed bears fruit and yields, in one case a hundredfold, in another sixty, and in another thirty.*" (Matthew 13:23) It's the same seed but in some it yields a lot more than in others. But that's just the way the Kingdom works. Jesus made this same point on numerous occasions. We never should compare the fruit of one believer against another. We are all different with our own unique spiritual giftedness, heritage, abilities, personality, experiences and destiny. You should want to produce all the fruit you can, making the most of your time, talents and opportunities, and leave the results up to the Lord. Jesus made this point crystal clear in the story of the three servants in Matthew 25:14-30.

A man entrusted his property to his three servants and

then left on a long journey. Each servant was given a different portion of his property to take care of *according to his ability.* (v15) This is a key phrase in the story. The man knew what his servants were capable of handling individually, so they were given responsibilities that matched their personal abilities. God knows your abilities because he chose to give you all of the skills, talents, opportunities and giftedness that you have. Stop worrying about what others are doing and focus on producing as much fruit in and through your life as you can. To live the abundant life Jesus came to give you, you must accept who you are and who you are not. Always strive to do your best, but leave the results up to God.

You have the opportunity to do the good works that God chose for you to do every day. Good works are not only the ways you serve at church or while participating in some ministry. All day long, at home, at work or at school, you and I have the opportunity to bear fruit in every good work. The Spirit led Paul to write *every.* A very literal translation of Colossians 1:10 is: *in every work good bearing fruit.* In every task and conversation, you can make it a good work that bears fruit as you are filled with the knowledge of God's will in all spiritual wisdom and in all spiritual understanding. You can speak life into a grocery store cashier who just had an irate customer. You can treat a co-worker like they matter more than anyone else. You can forgive the person who cut you off in traffic even though they will never know that you needed to forgive them. Out of the blue, you can let your wife know you cherish and adore her. You can tell your husband how much you respect the impeccable service he gives to his clients at work. You can teach your child why honesty is so important to God. We have opportunities every day and night to do the good works God has created us in Christ Jesus to do. And you can rest assured that the good works you do in Christ will always bear lasting, delicious fruit.

Each time you miss saying or doing the right thing, confess it quickly and ask your glorious Father to fill you with understanding of his will and his ways so that you will know how to respond the next time around. If the situation requires an apology from you, ask God to fill you with the wisdom of his will to know how to word it and when to speak it, so that he is acknowledged for his work in your spirit. Lasting fruit is the holy result of saying and doing what makes Jesus and the Father smile.

Result #3 - Growing in knowledge

The final result from asking your Father to fill you with the knowledge of his will is that you will continue: *growing in the knowledge of God.* (1:10c) You guessed it. The word for knowledge is that same compound word used in v9 and that was used in every other Kingdom Come Prayer. The result of this request is that we will keep growing in the full and complete knowledge of God.

Isn't it amazing that the God of the universe, Yahweh, who spoke everything into existence, wants us to know him fully and intimately? The more you ask to be filled with the understanding of what he wants you to say and do, the closer you and him become. If you think about it, it makes perfect sense.

What are we essentially doing when we ask the Father to fill us with the knowledge of his will in all spiritual wisdom and understanding? We are acknowledging our need of God. We are acknowledging that he has all the answers because he knows everything about everything. By regularly asking God to guide you to understand his will about what you are facing, you are acknowledging your dependence on him. Isn't life in Christ all about learning just how desperately dependent we are on him?

By asking God to fill you with his wisdom, you are also reminding yourself how much he loves you. Of course he wants to fill you with understanding through his Spirit. He loves you too much to do anything but that. Not only does he know the end from the beginning, he cares deeply about every detail of your life. Each time you ask the Father to fill you with the full knowledge of his will, you are also affirming your devotion to him. That makes the Father smile, it pleases the Spirit and it gives the Son great joy.

We not only produce fruit in other people's lives as we show them Jesus in flesh and blood through our words and actions, we actually grow more fruit within ourselves. More of the character of Jesus emerges. As we live a life of devotion and obedience that pleases the Father and produces fruit, we'll gain a deeper understanding of our heavenly Father. We'll understand more of his steadfast love for the world and his incredibly patient love for us. You will get to know your heavenly Father better as you actively engage in desiring to know his will. The prayer request comes full circle from asking to be filled with the knowledge of his will to growing in our personal knowledge of him. But you must act. You must begin praying, asking God to give you what he wants to give you, and expecting him to do so.

In *Amusing Ourselves to Death*, author Neil Postman wrote, "TV has habituated its viewers to a low information-action ratio, that people are accustomed to 'learning' good ideas (even from sermons and books) and doing nothing about them." You might be learning new ideas from this book and the many Scriptures we have considered. But learning, like faith, takes action to make it effective. You must put what you are learning to work. How will you begin to own these prayers for yourself? What are you going to do differently? You are probably aware of the definition of insanity: doing the same thing over and over again and expecting different results. It's time to get some new results through your praying.

Every challenge you face is a new opportunity to demonstrate your joyful confidence in your heavenly Father. Every blessing in your life is another opportunity for you to convey your love and appreciation for your place in his kingdom. Knowing God's will is how you recognize that everything good in your life has come directly from his hands. "Father in heaven, please fill me with the full knowledge of your will in all spiritual wisdom and understanding so that the way I live will be worthy of you, pleasing to you in every way, producing fruit in every action and thought, so that I will know you better and better. May it be so!"

Often times, you know exactly what the will of God is but lack the intestinal fortitude (guts) to do what you know is right. You know God doesn't want you to talk about other people, but when the conversation goes that direction, you just can't seem to resist joining in. You know it is against God's will to look at porn, but the urge seems too strong to resist and it's so available, right there on your desktop. What do you do in those cases?

REQUEST #2 - Strengthened with all power

May you be strengthened with all power, according to His glorious might. (Colossians 1:11a, HCSB) Some translations treat this verse as an additional result of the request in v9, to be filled with the knowledge of God's will. It is more practical, and it better aligns with the two prayers in Ephesians, to understand it as a second request. Neither is right or wrong. However, our need to be strengthened with God's power is obvious and on-going, which makes this request a particularly effective flare prayer.

This request closely parallels the request in Ephesians 3:16. Paul's wording in the Ephesian prayer is more descriptive: *that according to the riches of his glory he may grant you to be strengthened with power through his Spirit in your inner being.* In the Colossian prayer, the apostle is more direct, using exactly half the words to express the same need to be empowered. You get the feeling that he's in more of a hurry to get right to the central request. The poignancy and brevity of this powerful request is why I find myself repeating these words in the heat of the moment, when I'm in a pressing need of the Lord's strength. When you have the time, you brush your teeth to have nice fresh breath. But often, you only have time to pop in a piece of gum.

The Spirit led Paul, similar to how he led him in the Ephesian 3 prayer, to include the source of our empowerment: *according to His glorious might.* We can never give too much focus or emphasis on what God does for us. Remember how eloquently Paul described the power of God in raising Jesus from the dead in Ephesians 1:19-21? Let's look at that passage again. It is the third result of the first Kingdom Come Prayer, asking the Father to give his Spirit to help us know him better, flooding our hearts with the light of his Word. The third result of this request is so that we will know *the immeasurable greatness of his power toward us who believe, according to the working of his great might that he worked in Christ when he raised him from the dead and seated him at his right hand in the heavenly places, far above all rule and authority and power and dominion, and above every name that is named, not only in this age but also in the one to come.* What a fantastic description of the power of God that is available to us as his children. The power he can leverage in our lives is immeasurably great. There are no limits to its scope and reach. It is the same power that the Father exerted when he raised his Son back to life and gave him absolute and ultimate authority in the visible and invisible worlds. Is there anything his power can not accomplish in and through us?

Multiple words are necessary

As we have seen in these prayers, the apostle was so taken aback by the power of God that he used multiple words for power whenever he wrote about God's might. In the Colossian prayer, he asked for the believers to be empowered with all power according to God's strength. Paul was not able to write about God's power without using multiple words to try and describe it. What can we learn from this special phrasing inspired by the Holy Spirit?

Our need for the Father to strengthen us is greater than what we perceive. Our tendency, even as his redeemed people, is to revert back to the default attitude of most three year olds, "I'll do it myself." We simply fail to recognize how much strengthening is needed in order for us to stand firm in our faith, resisting the world, the flesh and the devil. To be strengthened with God's magnificent power will enable you to stand firm in the strong winds of trials, disappointments, setbacks and temptations. Through his power, you can live in the joy of your salvation even when it feels like all hell is breaking loose.

What is unique about this prayer request are the two results that come from it. These results help us to better understand how much of God's power we need each day.

Result #1 - Endurance and patience

May you be strengthened with all power, according to His glorious might, for all endurance and patience. (Colossians 1:11, HCSB) When you ask your heavenly Father to strengthen you, you will be empowered with all the endurance and all the patience you will need. What comes to your mind when you read "all endurance and patience"? What are you, or someone you dearly love, currently enduring? Who is trying your patience?

The quality and substance of your faith is tested every day. Stop and think about that. How was your faith tested yesterday? Did you stand firm in God's power? How did you endure that test? Did you rely on his strength in you? We all need his power to be able to endure life's trials as we patiently wait for the flood waters to subside.

My father-in-law recently completed treatment for larynx cancer. It was a horrible journey for him and his wife. Most of us know someone who has suffered through cancer treatment. The chemotherapy and radiation can produce side effects that make life almost unbearable. This is true for many other diseases as well. When we hear about someone being diagnosed with cancer, we immediately pray for healing, which is a loving thing to do. How do we pray for the Kingdom to come in the midst of cancer? There is no doubt that our loving, heavenly Father calls for some to suffer great hardships in life, whether it comes from cancer, the tragic loss of a child or a spouse, financial ruin - the sources of suffering seem endless. However, we can be confident in knowing the will of God when suffering comes. God may want to do something miraculous and suddenly end the pain. But he always wants to strengthen the person who is suffering so that they will have all the endurance and patience they need while at the same time never losing the joy of their place in his kingdom. His will is to empower us to persevere no matter how bad the circumstances are.

I vividly remember a past conversation with a young couple that had two small children. As the wife battled terminal cancer, they diligently looked for reasons why the Lord was allowing this illness. During treatments, they often had the opportunity to share with people the hope they had in Christ. Each conversation seemed to somehow justify their suffering. After many months of asking "Why Lord?", they accepted that God's plan was not to miraculously heal her. His plan was to empower them to be able to patiently endure this trial while clinging to the joy of their salvation. They realized that God had already done more for them in giving them salvation than he could ever do in healing the cancer. Rescuing people from the domain of darkness is the greatest thing that God can do for anyone. After months of treatments, the young woman went home to live with the Lord and her husband and children remained steadfast in their faith.

What endurance and patience do

A wonderful online Bible app is Blue Letter Bible. They define endurance as "in the NT (New Testament) the characteristic of a man who is not swerved from his deliberate purpose and his loyalty to faith and piety by even the greatest trials and sufferings." Patience is a very close synonym. Both words can also be translated steadfastness, constancy or endurance. The difference between these two words can be understood this way: endurance is what we need in tough circumstances and patience is what we need with trying people. That gives us a hook to hang these thoughts on as we pray.

You have and will continue to face many circumstances in your life that will require endurance. You know exactly what that feels like. Jesus never promised to rid us of heartaches and hardships; he promised to remain with us in the middle of those trials. It is in the tough times of life that we most need his enabling power. When the test shows it *is* cancer, when cut-backs are announced at work and when insurance won't cover the damage, we need spiritual strength to endure. When life is unfair, we need power from our Father to be able to persevere. God's power is there for the asking, to help you endure the trial so that you can get to know him better as you persevere.

We all have people in our lives who demand more patience than others. Marriage requires patience to endure and remain steadfast and true when the romance fades. If you have a middle schooler, you most definitely need enormous amounts of patience. The need for patience certainly doesn't fade as children become teens, it becomes a different kind of patience. So how do you show agape love to someone who demands more patience than you have a prescription for? Ask your heavenly Father, and keep asking, to empower you with all power (you might want to capitalize ALL when you pray) according to his glorious power so that you can show patience that only comes from the Father's might.

Henry Nouwen, in "A Spirituality of Waiting: Being Alert to God's Presence in Our Lives", *Weavings I*

(1986):9, wrote "The word patience means the willingness to stay where we are and live the situation out to the full in the belief that something hidden there will manifest itself to us. Impatient people are always expecting the real things to happen somewhere else and therefore want to go elsewhere. The moment is empty. But patient people dare to stay where they are." Have you ever felt that way about your church? Your marriage? Your job? The moment is empty. "There must be something better on the other side of the fence. Everything is happening somewhere else, but I'm stuck here." Those are feelings that many of us face. The solution is to ask the Father to strengthen you, or the person you are interceding for, to have the power needed to endure the situation, faithfully waiting on God and not forcing something to happen. Great is the reward for every follower of Jesus who perseveres under trials, remaining steadfast and faithful to Christ.

An inspiring example of a faithful man who was strengthened by God for all endurance and patience was Joseph. In Genesis 39-45 each part of his life story reveals another situation where Joseph's faith is tested. As a young man, he had to endure patiently as he suffered from hardships that others brought upon him. He quickly learned how to wait on God and trust in his hidden plan. A phrase that's repeated in his story tells the source of Joseph's strong faith: *the LORD was with him* (Genesis 39:2, 3, 21, 23).

Yahweh is with us as well, but in the New Covenant he is with us in a completely different way than in the first covenant. Now, the Spirit is *in* us, not just with us. He is leading, guiding and influencing our spirit. He will never leave us. The Holy Spirit dwells within us to empower us with all power so that we can faithfully endure every difficult situation and patiently love each challenging person. Our Father wants to empower us to be able to agape love others with all endurance and patience because that is how he loves us.

However, it's not a grit-your-teeth, white-knuckle kind of patient endurance that we are empowered with. When God is strengthening the person, endurance and patience are accompanied with joy.

Result #2 - Joy and thanksgiving

May you be strengthened with all power, according to His glorious might, for all endurance and patience with joy giving thanks to the Father, who has enabled you to share in the saints' inheritance in the light. (Colossians 1:11-12, HCSB) By God's power, the child of God is empowered to patiently endure with joy, not with anxiety or depression. This joy comes from the Spirit strengthening your heart and mind to realize that your sure hope is in God's salvation. He has chosen us by calling us out of the darkness and into his marvelous light. The Father decided to adopt us snotty-nosed, rebellious children, even though he knew we would not be as devoted to him as we should be. He has redeemed and forgiven us so that we can all equally participate in the inheritance of the saints in the light of the Kingdom of his dear Son.

The light of the kingdom is the righteous radiance of the Son of God shining into our hearts and minds the fullness of God himself. The light of the kingdom also points forward to the day when we will all have immortal bodies and live in the visible presence of Jesus and his Father, where there will be no need of a sun or moon because the radiance of their glory will be all the light we will need. (Revelation 21-22) Pretty cool, huh?

It is the Father himself who chose you, and made you

eligible. He enabled your adoption. You are qualified for the inheritance by God's grace and not because of anything you did. Jesus was very clear that nothing can ever steal your eligibility in the Kingdom. Even your worst sins, if you are indeed in Christ, cannot disqualify you from the Kingdom. God has called you into his family; nothing can ever separate you from his love. Anytime you need a reminder of this fact, read Romans 8:31-39 and soak in the truth of his steadfast love for you.

It's easy to think about how much God loves his people. The challenge comes when we imagine God loving us personally, because we know all the junk that still resides inside. For many of us, we don't feel worthy of his love, but this is a good thing because you never will be worthy of his love on your own. Therefore, rest in the power of his love because it is not dependent on your performance. Your good works are never the source of your forgiveness. Good works are the course of the forgiven. We do good deeds because God is making us good people, by his standards. Enduring patiently with joy is impossible without the empowering strength of the Spirit of God within your soul. Realize this truth and change the way you live by asking God daily to strengthen you with all power according to his glorious might.

Recharging batteries

Do you need power to overcome a habit? Do you need strength to press on in the ministry where you are serving? Is your joy meter on empty? Do you need his power to endure the continual partiality you are experiencing at work or at school? Do you need God's strength to be the spouse he has called you to be? Are the circumstances of your life robbing you of joy? Ask your Father for his help! Never stop asking him. Life in Christ is not a sprint; it's a marathon. About the time you feel like you have overcome one sin or trial, hang on, because another one is, very likely, right around the corner. Good news, huh? Yes, it is. It is fantastic news because you never have to face a trial or temptation alone. It is wonderful news because going through trials is precisely how you will come to know your own weaknesses and the power of God that is available to you, for the asking. Keep telling yourself what is true, what God says about you: *I can do all things through him who strengthens me.* (Philippians 4:13)

Spiritual recharging

If you are patiently enduring but you have little to no joy, ask your Father. When the joy of your salvation is missing or running low, it's because your power supply is depleted. Your spiritual batteries are almost out. The red bar is flashing "low battery". Do you recharge your cell phone every night? How much more does your spirit need recharging? The more you use your phone, the more frequently you need to recharge it. The more endurance and patience you need, the more you drain your spiritual power supply. Every challenge you face requires spiritual power from you. Every person who demands your patience drains your spiritual battery. Every temptation, discouraging remark, unloving response or disrespectful email depletes your spiritual strength and steals your joy. Recharging your spirit is critically important. How do you do that? Pray. Pray at least as often as you charge your phone. I don't mean as long, but at least as frequently as you plug it in. That might not be a bad place to start if you are not in the habit of conversing with your Father each day.

How long does it take your phone or tablet to be fully charged? How long should it take your spiritual batteries to be back at full power? If you are living off of occasional prayers or even a couple of flare prayers each day, you are missing out on what God wants to give you. Praying isn't about time, necessarily, but flare prayers must be coupled with times of quiet and reflective interaction with the Father using the outline given to us by his Son. Being *strengthened with all power, according to his glorious might* often happens as you are praying and reading the Bible. The three Epistles we have been studying all have amazing passages that will renew your spiritual energy and equip you to face anything that life might throw at you. Spending time reflecting on and praying through passages like John 6 and 15, Romans 7-8, Ephesians 1-2, Philippians 1-3 and Colossians 1-2 can bring you the renewed strength and encouragement that you need. Identifying favorite passages that rekindle your hope and reignite your joy will be one way the Father will renew your strength so that you can patiently endure the hard stuff of life without losing your joy.

The two verses that follow the prayer are a rich example of why we should be joyful and grateful: *He has rescued us from the domain of darkness and transferred us into the kingdom of the Son He loves. We have redemption, the forgiveness of sins, in Him.* (Colossians 1:13-14, HCSB) Why do you think Paul was led to write such profound truths to conclude his prayer? The explanation is found in the context of the passage. Studying the context of a passage is usually where we find the meaning of a verse or verses, and learn how to apply them to daily living. Let's look one more time at the context of this second request: *May you be strengthened with all power, according to His glorious might, for all endurance and patience, with joy giving thanks to the Father, who has enabled you to share in the saints' inheritance in the light. He has rescued us from the domain of darkness and transferred us into the kingdom of the Son He loves. We have redemption, the forgiveness of sins, in Him.* (vs11-14, HCSB)

Why do we give thanks to our Father? What is our source of joy? God has set us free! He sent his Son on the most dangerous rescue mission that has ever taken place for all of us, his people. Over the years, the Navy Seals have made hundreds of daring rescue missions. The *Finest Hour* is a powerfully inspirational movie about the most daring small-boat rescue the U.S. Coast Guard has ever made. Four men risked their lives in a frigid blizzard to save thirty three men from sinking oil tankers. Yet no military rescue mission can ever begin to compare to Jesus' rescue of human souls from the domain of darkness. We were held captive by sin, death and hell with no hope of being set free. Our redemption means that Jesus paid the ransom price to secure our freedom. The price was that all of our sins had to be credited to him, and he had to suffer in our place the judgment that we deserved.

Jesus did not suffer so that we would be happy. Happiness is fleeting. Jesus' came to give us joy - his very own joy in us. Having his joy doesn't mean we are never sad. Jesus wept at the tomb of his good friend Lazarus. Joy is much greater than happiness. Joy is the lasting emotion of knowing that our place in God's kingdom is secure. That God is in absolute control of the galaxies, the nations and your life is the source of your joy. Joy comes from knowing that God is with us and he will never leave us and that he loves us just the way we are, right now. However, he loves us so much that he will not leave us the way we are, right now. He will grow us up in our faith, and that means we must go through tough times. The joy of the Lord is knowing that we have been purchased for the Son and given to him, and that he will see us safely home. (John 6:35-40)

The joy of the Lord, being in relationship with him, is the source of our strength. If you have some gray hairs, you may have sung the children's song from Nehemiah 8:10, "The Joy of the Lord is My Strength." Rend Collective is an Irish praise, folk band that wrote a song about this same truth under the same title, "The Joy of the Lord is My Strength". Think through the lyrics and how they counter the challenges of life with joy and gratitude:

> Though tears may fall
> My song will rise, my song will rise to You
> Though my heart may fail
> My song will rise, my song will rise to You
> While there's breath in my lungs
> I will praise You, Lord
>
> In the dead of night
> I'll lift my eyes, I'll lift my eyes to You
> When the waters rise
> I'll lift my eyes, I'll lift my eyes to You
> While there's hope in my heart
> I will praise You, Lord
>
> The joy of the Lord is my strength
> The joy of the Lord is my strength
> In the darkness I'll dance
> In the shadows I'll sing
> The joy of the Lord is my strength
>
> When I cannot see You with my eyes
> Let faith arise to You

When I cannot feel Your hand in mine
Let faith arise to You
God of mercy and love
I will praise You, Lord

A dear friend called me last night to let me know his cancer had returned. He endured the harsh side effects of chemo and radiation treatments and then made it through a life-changing surgery. For a few months, he was cancer free. But now it's back. What does my friend need? Of course, friends and family are asking our Father to perform a miracle and make the cancer disappear. But how often does God really do that? His promise to us is not that we will live disease-free lives on this broken, sin-infested planet. No, we will get sick and suffer just like everyone else. But we can do it with joy. My friend's greatest need by far is to be strengthened with the power of God so that he can patiently endure this next journey with the authentic joy of knowing his place in the Kingdom. His wife, children and grandchildren also need God's power. He and his wife need to be filled with the knowledge of God's will with all wisdom and insights from the Spirit so they will know the right course of treatment to pursue for them.

Here is my Kingdom Come Prayer for them: "Dear Father, you know Rick and Jane's heart and soul and every cancer cell in his body. I ask that you will fill them with the clear understanding of what your will is when the treatment choices are presented. Bring them unity in that decision. Please fill them with your Spirit so they will know that you are with them and that you love them dearly. Please protect them from evil and the Evil One, so that they never doubt your love and your goodness. Strengthen this dear couple with all power, according to your glorious might so that they will be able to joyfully endure the journey that lies ahead for them, the journey of which only you know the full outcome. Empower them to remain steadfast in their faith so that their children, grandchildren, friends and neighbors can experience the deep joy that only you can give in a time like this. May their hearts and minds be focused on their gratefulness to you, because you have made them yours. Help them to focus on your grace and not on the cancer. Strengthen them to accept that your path for them includes this illness. Empower them in the depths of their souls to know you better through this trial and to know your strength to endure what they cannot bear on their own. Father, they are yours, so give them your Spirit so that they can know you more intimately and stand strong in the power of your might. May it be so."

When your joy is replaced by worry and sadness, cry out to your Father to empower you with all strength according to his glorious power so that you can know the full joy that rightfully belongs to you. Ask him, and keep on asking, to strengthen your mind and emotions to be able to overcome, by faith and with joy, your worries and sadness. Resolve in your heart that you want to know the joy of our Lord Jesus and you want others to see his joy in you. If you have determined to know his joy, you will diligently and consistently ask the Father to strengthen you accordingly. The great news is that he will do it. Because God is faithful and he loves you with a steadfast love, he will strengthen you with all of his might for all the endurance and patience you will need as you face life's challenges in the joy of the Lord.

May the God of hope fill you with all joy and peace as you trust in him, so that you may overflow with hope by the power of the Holy Spirit. (Romans 15:13, NIV)

Small Group Questions

1. What stands out to you the most in Colossians 1:9? What is the importance of "filled" and "all"?

2. Read Colossians 2:1-3. What exactly did Paul want to see happen? What do you see as the link between agape love and the knowledge of God's mystery?

3. What comes to your mind when you read *strengthened with all power* in 1:11? How do 1:29, Acts 4:33, Romans 15:13, 1 Corinthians 1:24 and 2:5, 2 Corinthians 4:7 and 12:9, Ephesians 3:7, 2 Thessalonians 1:11, 2 Timothy 1:7, and 1 Peter 1:5 picture the power of God?

4. When have you recently experienced the power of God in your life? How did it help you patiently endure?

5. Discuss specific ways that you can use these two prayer requests more frequently in your daily routine. When do you typically need to know God's will? Have his strength?

Close your time together by praying through this prayer as a group

Kingdom Come Prayer #4

Colossians 1:9-12

FIRST REQUEST

Father, fill me with the full knowledge of your will in all wisdom and spiritual understanding…

1st Result

so that the way I live will be worthy of you, fully pleasing you in every way…

2nd Result

so that I will produce fruit in every good thing I think, say and do…

3rd Result

increasing in my understanding of you.

SECOND REQUEST

Strengthen me with all power according to your glorious might…

1st Result

for all endurance and patience…

2nd Result

with joy, I'll thank you for making me eligible to share in the inheritance of the saints in light.

CHAPTER 7 - KINGDOM COME PRAYER #5 LOVING UNITY

The final Kingdom Come Prayer we will consider comes from the second half of the prayer Jesus prayed shortly before he was arrested on that Holy Thursday night. The old apostle John, probably well into his nineties, was led by the Spirit to write down these stories he had lived out and had been sharing with everyone who would listen for the past sixty years. Matthew, Mark and Luke's Gospels had long since been circulated among the churches, along with each of Paul's and Peter's letters. Can you picture John teaching from those letters and confirming everything that was written? He not only confirmed every story and all the truths recorded, he no doubt told his own stories to support and validate all the doctrines that Paul and Peter taught in their writings. John's account is so different from the other three, which are called the Synoptic Gospels, because the Holy Spirit wanted John to share his unique life experiences to give us more of Jesus' teaching and personal interaction with individuals. The three Synoptic Gospels stand as a unified witness and testimony that affirm each other's truthfulness. John's letter is an intimate account of Jesus' heart, of his love for his Father and his love for his followers. The old apostle was so overwhelmed as he wrote and reflected back on those three amazing years he spent with Jesus he concluded his letter declaring: *This is the disciple who is bearing witness about these things, and who has written these things, and we know that his testimony is true. Now there are also many other things that Jesus did. Were every one of them to be written, I suppose that the world itself could not contain the books that would be written.* (John 21:24-25) Can't you feel John's tension of wanting to write more and more about his beloved Master? Yet, we have all we will ever need, on this side of eternity.

The **Lord's Prayer**

Of all the incredible moments in Jesus' life that John was inspired to write about, there was one that stood out from all the rest. That is why almost twenty percent of John's account of Jesus' life and ministry comes from that Thursday night, the night before he was crucified, which is recorded in Chapters 13-17. The disciples had gathered together for the Jewish Passover meal in the upper room of a home in Jerusalem. After the meal, Jesus taught them spectacular truths about the Helper, the Spirit of truth, who would come in his place to be with them and to live in them. They apparently then left the room (14:31) to walk to one of Jesus' favorite places to pray, the Garden of Gethsemane. But he had much more to teach them. Along the way, Jesus must have stopped beside a vineyard to make a powerful and pertinent illustration (15:1-17) about staying connected to him and that launched him into further teaching about the Holy Spirit (15:18-16:33). Imagine standing with

Jesus on that dark night, hearing him say for the fifth time that evening: "*These things I command you, so that you will love one another.*" (15:17) What Jesus did next is profound.

He turned his gaze from the eleven to his Father in the heavens. He looked up into the night sky as if he was looking directly into his Father's eyes, then he prayed. Chapter 17 is indeed the Lord's Prayer. It is Jesus' prayer for the Kingdom of God to come on earth, as it is in heaven. First, he prayed for the eleven disciples who were standing there with him, watching and listening to every word he spoke. Can you imagine what Peter, Andrew, James, Matthew and the others were thinking that night as they listened to Jesus pray? Can you picture being in a church service where the old apostle John is retelling exactly how it all happened? Can you hear the passion in his voice?

In 17:20, Jesus changed the focus of his prayer. He transitioned from praying for the eleven to praying for you and me! He had in his heart and mind every believer, from that point in time forward, who would receive the fantastic news of forgiveness of sins by believing in who he is. I wonder if he could picture our faces or see this vast army of future followers who would come from every nation, tribe and language. This is the Lord's Prayer for you and me and all who call on the name of the Lord.

> "*I do not ask for these only, but also for those who will believe in me through their word, that they may all be one, just as you, Father, are in me, and I in you, that they also may be in us, so that the world may believe that you have sent me. The glory that you have given me I have given to them, that they may be one even as we are one, I in them and you in me, that they may become*

> *perfectly one, so that the world may know that you sent me and loved them even as you loved me. Father, I desire that they also, whom you have given me, may be with me where I am, to see my glory that you have given me because you loved me before the foundation of the world. O righteous Father, even though the world does not know you, I know you, and these know that you have sent me. I made known to them your name, and I will continue to make it known, that the love with which you have loved me may be in them, and I in them.*" (John 17:20-26)

After he finished praying, he led them across the brook Kidron, into the Garden of Gethsemane. Once there, he encouraged them to pray while he went by himself to a private corner of the garden to speak some very passionate prayers to his loving Father. (Matthew 26:36-46; Mark 14:32-42; Luke 22:39-46) Let's now look at Jesus' prayer for his people to understand what his requests mean for you and me.

Jesus' request for unity

Jesus asked his Father for two things. The first request is *that they may all be one, just as you, Father, are in me, and I in you, that they also may be in us.* (17:21a) What a prayer! Did the Father answer his Son's request? Yes! The divine mystery of God's plan for mankind was that through his Son's atoning sacrifice and resurrection, the New Covenant was ratified. God could now give his people a new heart and a new spirit and be in them forever, as Jesus promised. God can only have righteous people as his children. Through Jesus' atoning sacrifice, our unrighteousness is taken away forever and replaced with the righteousness of Jesus himself. That is the only way that we can be in Christ and he can be in us. It is a world-shattering concept to believe that we are in Jesus and in the Father and that they are in us. But that is exactly what Jesus made possible. By his grace and through our faith, we are not only forgiven, we are completely in Christ. Our new identification is in him. There are so many verses that declare this reality. This is what Jesus was illustrating with the vine and the branches just a few minutes earlier. I realize that much of the time we don't feel like we are in Christ or that the Father is in us. We often feel like everyone else - that we're just plugging away at life, trying not to mess things up too badly. The amazing reality is, however, that God has made us his own and has given us to his Son. That's the new creation that you are. Your new and forever identity is that you belong to the Father through the Son.

Jesus repeated the request with even greater passion: *The glory that you have given me I have given to them, that they may be one even as we are one, I in them and you in me, that they may become perfectly one.* (17:22-23a) What was the glory that Jesus gave to his followers? It was the mystery of God's plan of redemption for all mankind. Through his Son's obedience, he would reconcile rebellious people to himself and to one another. We are not given new information about God and forgiveness, we are given a new heart and soul. Red and yellow, black and white, brown and cream are precious too. We are all equally brought into a new and vibrant relationship with the Father so that we can be his people throughout an endless age, just as he always wanted it to be.

Jesus' request was most definitely answered. The dividing walls that separated people by race, language, education, status, power, positions, ranking and talents were obliterated by Jesus' atoning sacrifice. No believer is better than any other believer and no believer is inferior to any other believer. Our new life is in stark contrast to our old life. Without Christ: jobs, education, talents, abilities, experiences, personality, the neighborhood or country you live in, the sorority you belong to, the school you attend, the color of your skin - they all separate us from each other with an ungodly grading system of determining who is the least and most important. All of those dividers are part of the sin-saturated world we live in. What sets all of Jesus' followers apart is the fact that we belong to him, we are in him and his Spirit lives within us. He is our life!

The Spirit is our guarantee, similar to a wedding ring. The rings we wear are proof that we have committed ourselves to our spouse for the rest of our lives. The Spirit living within us is the proof that we belong to the Lord Jesus Christ and will live with him in the new heaven and new earth for an ageless age: *In him you also, when you heard the word of truth, the gospel of your salvation, and believed in him, were sealed with the promised Holy Spirit, who is the guarantee of our inheritance until we acquire possession of it, to the praise of his glory.* (Ephesians 1:13-14) You hopefully recognized this verse which precedes Kingdom Come Prayer #1 in Ephesians 1 (Chapter 3 of this book). This truth is definitely worth repeating. This helps us to understand that what Jesus prayed that night was answered through the cross and is being answered every day as more and more people enter the Kingdom through receiving the Lord Jesus into their lives.

Notice that Jesus asked that the same intimacy that he and his Father enjoy be shared with all believers. It is an amazing prayer that we can't fully comprehend on this side of eternity. What we can understand is that there is no place for prejudice or any other division in the Kingdom. Jesus' prayer was answered by the Father. He brought us all into the Kingdom of his dear Son, and that is a fact. What is left for us to do is to live in this truth that Jesus made possible.

Unity in diversity

The problem is that we don't often live in this reality. Too frequently, we hold onto the things that divide us. I have prejudices and so do you. You still allow your old ways of showing partiality to leak through and so do I. The fact that we struggle living out this unity shows us how much we need to ask God to strengthen us with his power. Kingdom Come Prayer #2 from Ephesians 3:16-19 (Chapter 4 of this book) is the answer to bringing healing when divisions have caused heartache. The most important good work that every follower of Jesus is to be about is focusing on the One who unites us, who is infinitely greater than all that divides us.

How much does God appreciate diversity? Why did it bring him glory to create different ethnicities, languages and people groups? Diversity gives God glory. His creativity is witnessed throughout creation. How many shades of green are there? Why did God choose to create so many different green hues? It gave him pleasure. It enriches our lives. The differences in people are directly from the hand of God and, as his people, we must learn to celebrate our unique differences. From the poorest of the poor to the wealthiest apprentice of Jesus alive today, we are absolutely equal before our great Creator. To every soul King David testified:

> *For you created my inmost being;*
> *you knit me together in my mother's womb.*
> *I praise you because I am fearfully and wonderfully made;*
> *your works are wonderful,*
> *I know that full well.* (Psalm 139:13-14, NIV)

Jesus ended his prayer with these words: "*I made known to them your name, and I will continue to make it known, that the love with which you have loved me may be in them, and I in them.*" (John 17:26) When Jesus said he would continue to make the Father's name known, he meant that he would continue to reveal everything about who the Father is and what he is like. This is what he is doing in and through us, every day of our lives. Jesus is interceding for us that we would come to know the Father in all of his fullness. Jesus promised his Father that he would never stop teaching his people all about him so that the same love the Father has for the Son will be in all of us. And the Lord Jesus will be in us, through his Spirit. Through the power of the Spirit in us, we can experience the same agape love that the Father gives to his Son. He has always loved us this way. Working out our salvation means we are striving, with his strength, to agape love each other in spite of all our differences. Agape love is so paramount to our faith in Jesus that he repeated the command to his disciples that Thursday night five times. Five times! Then they heard it again in his prayer. If there is a summary statement of faith in Christ for us to follow it is this: Agape love one another!

It is most interesting that I am writing this chapter on Wednesday morning, Nov. 9, 2016. Donald Trump has just won the presidency. Sadly, the election was very divisive for Jesus' people. This morning, many believers are praising God and giving him credit for the results. Facebook and Instagram are full of people praising God for Trump's win. Other believers are deeply saddened, some are fearful, and others are angry as they wonder why God didn't answer their prayers. Much of the division is racial. The majority of blacks and Hispanics voted for Hillary Clinton while the majority of whites voted for Donald Trump. How will we ever unite his Church under these circumstances? How can Jesus' prayer be experienced on earth like it is in heaven? By the grace of God! It is the work of every follower of Jesus, especially in the U.S., to focus on Who unites us rather than on all the things that divide us. Of course, we're going to have different opinions about how the government should operate, the programs that are offered, tax reform, health care, college education and immigration. If we all agreed, some of us wouldn't be needed! As Jesus' people, we must learn how to disagree agreeably. Listening to each other is so important to diminishing prejudices. "Listen to learn" might be a worthy personal mantra for each of us to embrace. We have to prayerfully work out our salvation by not allowing the non-essentials to come between us. The One who unites us is infinitely greater than all that divides us. And there is so much at stake!

The impact of loving unity

We have been made one in Christ and now we must live out that unity "*so that the world may believe that you have sent me.*" (17:21b) This is so critical that Jesus then repeated this result in 17:23b: "*so that the world may know that you sent me and loved them even as you loved me.*" The Church's history makes it difficult for the world to believe that Jesus has rescued and transformed us. But let's focus on the here and now and what you and I can do to live out this holy unity that we have been so graciously given. Your friends, neighbors and co-workers need to see this unity that is shared among all Christ-followers so that they can believe in him too. How do we do that?

Pray! The Father wants to help you by giving you his

Spirit's wisdom, power and love. That is what we have learned from the Kingdom Come Prayers. If you peel them all back you will see that we are to continually ask our Father to give us his wisdom, power and love and it will come through his Spirit who lives in us. Agape love is not only possible, it is what our Father expects from us every day. When we fail to agape love, he expects us to confess our sins, repent of them and go out and agape love better.

You can agape love any fellow follower of Jesus by striving to understand them better. With God's help, you can get to know them so that you can better relate to how they feel, why they voted the way they did, what their fears are and what they value. Learn to understand their heritage and their home life so that you can identify, at least to some degree, what it's like living in their shoes. Our white pastor just told a story about meeting with a black pastor at a local coffee shop. They both wanted to build a friendship to see how the two churches might experience more of the unity that is theirs in Christ. As they talked, the black pastor asked my pastor if he perceived anything unique about their surroundings. My pastor couldn't think of anything that jumped out to him. The black pastor pointed out that since they had arrived, he was the only black person in the entire coffee shop.

Agape love will always cost you. That is why Jesus described our lives as his followers this way: "*If anyone would come after me, let him deny himself and take up his cross daily and follow me.*" (Luke 9:23) We are being transformed into the kind of people who don't demand their way. That's revolutionary in our world of entitlements and victimization. To deny yourself, take up your cross, and die daily means you will strive first to understand, rather than making sure you are understood. You will work at listening, by God's grace and strength, rather than making sure you are heard. All of the other Kingdom Come Prayers will come into play in living out agape love. As you lean in towards a fellow follower from another race or socio-economic background, ask the Father to make your agape love overflow more and more so that you can truly listen and empathize. That person is a sinner-made-saint just like you, but with uniquely different Spiritual gifts, heritage, abilities, personality, experiences and destiny. No follower of Jesus is better than any other one. We are all one in Christ and we are all equal in Christ.

Unity among believers

A number of the churches in New Testament times were struggling with unity, exactly like we do in our churches today. Living by agape love in the unity that is ours as his people has always been a challenge for some churches. Our failure to agape love shows us how much we need him daily and how important the Kingdom Come Prayers are to our churches and our families. The church in Corinth was torn apart by all kinds of divisions. They were one in Christ spiritually, but in practice, they divided themselves according to heritage, income, giftedness and leader preferences (Paul, Apollos or Jesus). The Spirit inspired Paul to address the divisions head-on, especially in 1 Corinthians 12-14. Sandwiched in the middle of these chapters is the infamous Chapter 13, the "Love Chapter" (pages 149-150) that is often quoted at weddings. Paul's answer to the division problem was agape love. Agape love is the answer to virtually all of the problems that plague our relationships. Paul also encouraged the Ephesian believers to live in the unity that Jesus purchased for them: *Therefore I, the prisoner for the Lord, urge you to walk worthy of the calling you have received, with all humility and gentleness, with patience, accepting one another in love, diligently keeping the unity of the Spirit with the peace that binds us. There is one body and one Spirit — just as you were called to one hope at your calling — one Lord, one faith, one baptism, one God and Father of all, who is above all and through all and in all.* (Ephesians 4:1-6, HCSB) Our calling as Jesus' people is to be very diligent to live out the unity of the Spirit that is ours in Christ. If we will deny our self-centered tendencies, work diligently and pray consistently, we can experience the peace that binds us together. If Jesus is more and more at home in your heart (first result of KCP #2), then you will be able to focus more on the One who unites us rather than the many differences that separate us.

You can lead the way in your church, in your neighborhood, at your school or work. You can begin to reach out to those who are different than you, to agape love them, because you are one in Christ. Know this. Anytime you are part of creating divisions in your church, class or small group, you are sinning against Jesus and what he accomplished in us through the cross. Do nothing to divide what Jesus united! When you throw stones at another church, you are dividing what Christ has already united. When you complain about the music or the messages or the children's curriculum, you are bringing division to what Jesus died to unite. Stop, drop and pray. Change your attitude and actions to diligently keep the unity of the Spirit among all of those you know who have trusted in Jesus for the forgiveness of sins. What are you to do if they are not acting like Jesus' redeemed people? Agape love and forgive them anyway. The chances are quite high that others will need to forgive you in a similar way.

Denominations are going to exist. That's not a bad thing, as long as we emphasize the One who unites us all. God loves diversity; look at all of our differences as humans. As we have considered earlier in this chapter, God is creative; how many nose shapes did he create? The error comes when we begin to think our nose, or denomination, or our style of praise music or our way of worshipping is superior – that it's the Bible way. That kind of thinking comes from a big dose of pride on a triple shot espresso high. We must learn to jettison that prideful kind of stinkin' thinkin'! Jesus' abundant life is living in the unity that he has created by giving us all the same hope, the same Spirit, the same Lord, the same faith, the same baptism and the same God and Father of us all. But Jesus' prayer for unity was coupled with another passionate request.

Jesus' request for us to be with him

Father, I desire that they also, whom you have given me, may be with me where I am, to see my glory that you have given me because you loved me before the foundation of the world. (John 17:24) Jesus had no glory on earth. He laid his former glory to the aside to come to earth as a human, to be one of us. When he was only a few hours from completing his work on earth, Jesus looked ahead to what was coming. Even when facing inexplicable suffering, Jesus was thinking about us and looking forward to when we all will live with him, in the visible presence of his breath-taking glory. This is such a tender moment between a Father and Son. The Son's deep desire is for everyone who will believe in him to be able to experience the wonder and power of his presence. This request, like the first one, is already answered. It will take place. Millions of saints are basking in the radiance of his glory at this very moment. We will all be there soon enough.

John got to actually see a glimpse of Jesus' former glory. One day, Jesus took him, Peter and John's brother, James, on a high mountain to pray. As he was praying: *He was transformed in front of them, and His face shone like the sun. Even His clothes became as white as the light.* (Matthew 17:2, HCSB) Remember, when John wrote his account of Jesus' life and ministry, he was most likely in his nineties. He was probably around thirty years old when he witnessed Jesus' transfiguration. Imagine how many times John told that story. He had no need of including it in his written account because everyone had been reading about it for years in the accounts written by Matthew, Mark and Luke. Since John saw it all in person, no doubt he often described it to his listeners. Here, as he wrote out the prayer they had heard Jesus pray that fateful Thursday night, surely he had a flashback to that euphoric mountaintop experience. We are not sure if John wrote his Gospel account before or after he wrote the Revelation. Either way, John was given the holy privilege of seeing Jesus in his glory another time, when the Lord appeared to him on the island of Patmos.

It is challenging for you and me to picture Jesus' glory. He knows that. I believe that is one reason the Spirit inspired John to describe what Jesus looked like when Jesus appeared to him during his exile on the island of Patmos.

> *Then I turned to see the voice that was speaking to me, and on turning I saw seven golden lampstands, and in the midst of the lampstands one like a son of man, clothed with a long robe and with a golden sash around his chest. The hairs of his head were white, like white wool, like*

> *snow. His eyes were like a flame of fire, his feet were like burnished bronze, refined in a furnace, and his voice was like the roar of many waters. In his right hand he held seven stars, from his mouth came a sharp two-edged sword, and his face was like the sun shining in full strength.*
>
> *When I saw him, I fell at his feet as though dead. But he laid his right hand on me, saying, "Fear not, I am the first and the last, and the living one. I died, and behold I am alive forevermore, and I have the keys of Death and Hades. Write therefore the things that you have seen, those that are and those that are to take place after this. As for the mystery of the seven stars that you saw in my right hand, and the seven golden lampstands, the seven stars are the angels of the seven churches, and the seven lampstands are the seven churches."* (Revelation 1:12-20)

Read through this description a few times. Close your eyes and try to imagine Jesus' dazzling, snow-white hair, his eyes of a warm, alluring fire, beautifully bronzed feet and a voice that boomed like Niagara Falls. John was terrified at Jesus' glory and all but passed out. Then Jesus lovingly reached out and touched him to assure him that he had nothing to fear. There are two ways you can think about *eyes like a flame of fire*. For those who have rejected Jesus as their Master, those eyes are a terrifying flame of judgment, but for his people, they are the eyes of a warm, inviting fire that you can't stop staring into. You've sat in front of fires like that, eyes mesmerized by the warm, flickering flames, haven't you?

For those who are nearing the end of their life on earth, let them know Jesus has already prayed for them to be with him where he is so that they can experience his glory. For all believers who are dealing with terminal illnesses, the thought that Jesus wants them to come home to be with him and to enjoy his glory is the vision they need to cling to. We can pray for them in this way.

But the vision of living in the visible presence of Jesus and the Father is one that we all can learn to cling to. We can't think about heaven too much. The phrase that someone is so heavenly minded that they are no earthly good is a smoke laden lie from the pit of hell. As we read from Colossians 3:1-4 on page 169, we are instructed to set our minds and our emotions on where Jesus is and what he is doing. The more effective you are at maintaining a heavenly perspective, the more balanced your earthly priorities become. And this is accomplished through persistent Kingdom Come Praying.

What is our part in fulfilling Jesus' prayer? We can live in agape love as one Church when we determine that we will, as individuals and as his local church, work out our salvation with fear and trembling. In closing, let's return to Philippians 2:12-13: *Therefore, my beloved, as you have always obeyed, so now, not only as in my presence but much more in my absence, work out your own salvation with fear and trembling, for it is God who works in you, both to will and to work for his good pleasure.* Learning to own the Kingdom Come Prayers and use them each day is how you can successfully work out your own salvation with fear and trembling. Why fear and trembling?

We should tremble in fear because we have such a great propensity to revert back to our old ways, to how we thought before we knew God. "Prone to wander Lord I feel it, prone to leave the God I love" is such a poignant verse from the hymn, "Come Thou Fount of Every Blessing." It takes supernatural power to love Jesus and obey everything that he commanded. The only way to be strong in the Lord, so that you can obey him, is to realize how weak and vulnerable you really are.

There should also be a holy dread of disappointing God and grieving the Holy Spirit. Wouldn't your life be more enjoyable if you kept a healthy fear of failing to be the salt and light of the earth? We should be somewhat anxious that our lives may turn someone away from Jesus rather than draw them to him. I want to maintain a healthful dread of denying my Lord. I want to be afraid that I might not live up to his calling.

The last part of this passage is especially encouraging. You need not be worried or anxious about your life's choices as long as you live in the reality of your own potential because *it is God who works in you, both to will and to work for his good pleasure.* The NLT translated it: *For God is working in you, giving you the desire and the power to do what pleases him.* Ah, that's it. That's the answer to your weaknesses. God is working in you. He is giving you both the desires of his heart and the strength of his Spirit. How do you make sure you remain aligned with his desires and strength? Ask him. Ask him according to his will, which is his Word, from the Kingdom Come Prayers, to fill you with his Spirit's wisdom and power and agape love. Own these prayers as you put Jesus' prayer outline to work and the way you live will be worthy of the Lord, fully pleasing him and producing fruit in every good action and thought, growing deeper in your intimate knowledge of your Father in the heavens.

All four Kingdom Come Prayers are summarized on pages 231-232. This book is designed so that you can cut out that page, as well as the single pages of the four prayers (pages 91, 137, 165 and 209), so that you can keep them with you. If you don't especially like the English Standard Version (ESV), then use whatever translation you prefer. Work out your salvation by working these prayers into your heart and mind. Learn to ask God for what he most definitely wants to give you, his wise and powerful Spirit.

Remember, you can develop a vibrant relationship with God through your regular conversations with him. You will need to have extended conversations, using Jesus' prayer outline, where you can spend significant time thinking and listening. Throughout the day, you will need to launch Kingdom Come Flare Prayers on demand as you need the Spirit's insights, power and agape love. Determine that you are going to stand strong in the Lord and in the strength of his might by disciplining yourself to deepen your conversations with your Father in the heavens. And when you fail, and you will, confess your failures and resolve anew to grow in your understanding of God's Word and his ways. You can do this through Christ who empowers you. God is constantly giving you both the desire and the ability to do what pleases him. Have the same mindset that Jesus had, to honor our Father in everything and in every way.

> *I write these things to you who believe in the name of the Son of God, that you may know that you have eternal life. And this is the confidence that we have toward him, that if we ask anything according to his will he hears us. And if we know that he hears us in whatever we ask, we know that we have the requests that we have asked of him.* (1 John 5:13-15)
>
> *Now to him who is able to do far more abundantly than all that we ask or think, according to the power at work within us, to him be glory in the church and in Christ Jesus throughout all generations, forever and ever. Amen.* (Ephesians 3:20-21)

May it be so for you, your church family, and everyone you know who belongs to Christ Jesus!

Small Group Questions

1. Picture Jesus standing by a vineyard with the eleven gathered around him in the dark, looking up into heaven and read John 17:1-26. Discuss what stands out to you the most in his prayer.

2. What do you think it looks like today for a group of believers to demonstrate the unity that Jesus purchased for us? See Acts 2:42-47 and 4:32-37.

3. Read Ephesians 4:1-6. What is required from every believer in order to walk worthy of our calling? What is the practical significance for us today in vs4-6?

4. Read again how Jesus finished this momentous prayer (vs26-27). What is Jesus doing now? Why? How can each of us fully participate in what Jesus is doing?

5. Encourage each other with how you are using the Followers' Prayer Outline and the Kingdom Come Prayers. What results have you seen from using this outline and these prayers?

Kingdom Come Prayer #1 Ephesians 1:17-19

THE REQUEST I ask you, the glorious Father of my Lord Jesus Christ, to give me your Spirit who has all wisdom and revelation, to help me know you more fully, having my heart flooded with your light…

1st Result

so that I might know what is the hope of your calling…

2nd Result

so that I might know what are the riches of your glorious inheritance in the saints…

3rd Result

so that I might know what is the immeasurable greatness of your power toward us who believe.

Kingdom Come Prayer #2 Ephesians 3:16-19

THE REQUEST Dear Father in the heavens, I ask that out of your glorious riches, you will grant me to be strengthened with your power, through your Spirit, in my core…

1st Result

so that Jesus will be more at home in my heart through faith, being rooted and grounded in agape love…

2nd Result

so that I'll have strength to understand, with all fellow believers, how wide and high and long and deep Jesus' love is, experiencing it beyond just knowledge…

3rd Result

so that together, we might be filled with all of your fullness.

Kingdom Come Prayer #3 Philippians 1:9-11

THE REQUEST Father, make my agape love overflow more and more in full knowledge and all discernment…

1st Result

so that I can determine what is excellent and be pure and blameless until the day of Christ…

2nd Result

so that I can be filled with the fruit of righteousness that comes through Jesus Christ, to your glory and praise.

Kingdom Come Prayer #4 Colossians 1:9-12

FIRST REQUEST Father, fill me with the full knowledge of your will in all wisdom and spiritual understanding…

1st Result

so that the way I live will be worthy of you, fully pleasing you in every way…

2nd Result

so that I will produce fruit in every good work

3rd Result

increasing in my understanding of you.

SECOND REQUEST

Strengthen me with all power according to your glorious might…

1st Result

for all endurance and patience…

2nd Result

with joy, I'll thank you for making me eligible to share in the inheritance of the saints in light.

ABOUT THE AUTHOR

Bill Simpson serves as the Founder and Executive Director of Pidea Alliance Inc., a 501(c)(3) bringing Released Time Bible Education classes to the public school students of southeastern NC. He and his wife, Tammy, both grew up in Fuquay-Varina, NC. They were married shortly after Bill graduated from NC State's School of Engineering in 1981. A few months after their marriage, Bill became a follower of Jesus. After 8 years of success in business, the Simpsons realized the Lord was leading them in an entirely new direction. They sold their home and company in order for Bill to attend seminary at Columbia International University in Columbia, SC. After graduation, they ministered as church planters for six years in Senegal, West Africa with the mission organization, SIM. Bill's first book was an explanation of practical theology written in Wolof, the primary language of Senegal. When the Simpsons returned to the US in 1997, Bill was privileged to serve as the Senior Pastor of their home church in High Point, NC, Community Bible Church. He ministered there for almost 10 years and then returned to the marketplace. Over the next 5 years, he held positions in leadership consulting and energy conservation. Bill and Tammy were led back into the pastorate in March of 2012, as he became the Lead Pastor of Manchester Creek Community Church in Rock Hill, SC. While there, Bill joined the board of a new nonprofit organization where he learned about Released Time Bible Education and this unprecedented opportunity to offer public school students a values-based, Christ-centered, character development, educational experience. Bill resigned from Manchester Creek in July 2016 to launch Pidea Alliance Inc. "Pidea" comes from the Greek word that means to educate, guide, nurture, train and instruct. To learn more, please visit Pidea Alliance Inc. at www.PideaAlliance.org.

65959120R00145

Made in the USA
Charleston, SC
08 January 2017